A Pizza The Action

Also by Christopher Carosa…

Hey! What's My Number? – The One Thing Every Retirement Investor Wants and Needs to Know

50 Hidden Gems of Greater Western New York – A handbook for those too proud to believe "wide right" and "no goal" define us.

401(k) Fiduciary Solutions – Expert Guidance for 401(k) Plan Sponsors on how to Effectively and Safely Manage Plan Compliance and Investments by Sharing the Fiduciary Burden with Experienced Professionals

Due Diligence – The Individual Trustee's Guide to Selecting and Monitoring a Professional Money Manager

A Pizza The Action

- or -

Everything I Ever Learned About Business I Learned by
Working in a Pizza Stand at the Erie County Fair

Christopher Carosa

This book contains both original and previously published work. Some material contained herein represents the opinions of the individuals quoted and not necessarily the opinion of the author. In some cases, for metaphorical purposes, this work contains fiction. In such circumstances, names, characters, places and incidents are either the product of the author's imagination or are used fictitiously. Any resemblance to actual events or locales or persons, living or dead, is entirely coincidental.

Limit of Liability/Disclaimer of Warranty: While the publisher and the author have used their best efforts in preparing this book, they make no representations or warranties with respect to the accuracy or completeness of the contents of this book and specifically disclaim any implied warranties or merchantability or fitness for any particular purpose. No warranty may be created or extended by sales representatives or written sales materials. If you actually read this, go to "X" in the Index right now.

To my grandparents, without whom this book could never have been written.

And to their grandchildren and great-grandchildren (and beyond), many being too young to have experienced our grandparents the way my brother and I did.

CONTENTS

Part I - A Day in the Life of a Carny

Part II - Personal Values

Part III - Community Values

Part IV - Business Values

Part V - Life's Launching Pad

Part VI - Appendix

FOREWORD

Many business books provide examples of complicated management scenarios in an attempt to teach their readers how to be successful entrepreneurs. The authors of these books seem to suggest that good entrepreneurs must somehow be blessed with a unique skill set or the ability to learn from complex business situations.

Chris Carosa has provided the opposite view. He demonstrates how his entrepreneurial training came from the simple, yet crucial, life lessons he learned as a young man working in his grandparents' pizza stand at the Erie County Fair. (My side note: I recall visiting the Erie County Fair frequently as a child and young adult. Chris' stories brought back some fond and some not-so-fond memories, especially as a customer of the "carnies.")

As he makes clear through his lively prose, Chris' grandparents were not formally educated entrepreneurs, but, rather, hard-working blue collar folks with real life skills and common sense. It is the basic lessons he learned from them that translate so perfectly for many business situations.

Chris utilizes a series of vignettes to provide, in a self-effacing style, very thoughtful examples of how hard work, coupled with solid personal, family, community, and business values, are the basis from which strong managers and entrepreneurs can succeed. Chris' description of the twenty hour days, the core principles learned from his grandparents, the long term development of interpersonal relationships, and willingness to watch and learn, yet sometimes, step out on his own, provides the reader a wonderful process to learn these basic building blocks.

Chris gives the reader 54 Lessons that he has followed in his entrepreneurial ventures. Lesson #54 sums up my view on Chris: "If You Learn the Right Lessons, Sometimes You Can Return a Favor in Ways You Never Imagined." Chris not only tells some wonderful stories, but for many of us, he brings back some long lost memories.

Jeff Glajch
Chief Financial Officer
Graham Corporation
Batavia, New York
July 26, 2014

PREFACE

When I wrote *50 Hidden Gems of Greater Western New York*, I knew I just had to include a chapter on the Erie County Fair. Naturally, if I was to write about the Erie County Fair, then I also had to include some mention of my grandparents' pizza stand (then called Salvator's Pizza – across from what used to be the main entrance of the grandstand). And so I did. In that chapter (you can read it in the appendix section of this book) I mentioned the lessons learned in that pizza stand would make a wonderful book.

This is that book.

Even the simplest of life's activities can build the most enduring memories. More important, in subtle ways they can offer lessons that stand a lifetime. When fully absorbed, these lessons can yield powerful results. In his book *One Up On Wall Street*, Fidelity's superstar investor Peter Lynch explains how everyday investors can profit just by paying attention to the companies in their own backyard. Similarly, it is these same "backyard" (and sometime front yard) experiences of our youth that provide the lessons needed to reach the highest of heights in the business world. Much has been written of the proverbial lemonade stand and how it teaches budding entrepreneurs the meaning of business. This book takes place in the real-life world of a small family-owned and operated pizza stand in one of America's most popular and prosperous annual fairs – the Erie County Fair – and follows through the events that led a young adult to learn invaluable lessons that, in the future, would help him become a successful entrepreneur.

As with any memoir-like book, many of the events depicted in this book are subject to interpretation. I've tried to keep true to what I saw as a teenager back then, not what I know to be true today. This is important because, when you learn lessons, certain small aspects stick out. In retrospect, those aspects might be irrelevant to the full story or even the main point of the story. And yet, that's what you remember, because that's the lesson you learn.

The stories I've told here reflect the lessons I learned. My brother (or my sisters or my aunt and uncles) might have experienced the same event and learned a different lesson and therefore remembered a different aspect of that event. This book isn't their story, it's mine. That being said…

I've loaded this book with quick-read chapters containing real-life episodes from that time of my life (roughly 1974 to 1983). The book is divided into five sections with a prologue and an epilogue (and one appendix). I introduce the key players in the short prologue through a story that happens about as far from the Erie County Fair as possible. The first section – A Day In the Life of a Carny – takes you on an speedy journey through a typical day I spent working in the pizza stand. The next three sections introduce you to the lessons and values learned during this time. The first of these three identifies basic values, the next reveals community values and the following section pinpoints business values. These sections are organized to not only give you both a flavor and feel of what was happening at the time these stories occured, but to make it clear where the lessons learned appear in your life. The final section shows how I used these lessons by describing five essential elements to success. Lastly, the epilogue tries to answer the obvious "What happened to them?" questions that generally come about when discussing the past lives of characters (think of the endings of *American Graffiti*, *Animal House*, and *Fast Times at Ridgemont High*).

Chris Carosa
Mendon, New York
July 15, 2014

ACKNOWLEDGEMENTS

As with any book, this one owes a great deal to many people, including my entire family. It starts with my grandparents, whose wisdom, understanding, and genuine concern all played an essential part to what eventually became this book. I'd especially like to thank my parents and my brother and sisters, all of whom helped voluminously with the content editing (in particular, my brother Kenny, who helped me remember some of the events time has eroded from my memory). Actually, I really do want to thank Kenny, who was there at the creation – with me helping my grandparents during the late 1970s and early 1980s. He made the experience all the more fun.

Of course, my aunt and uncles also played a critical role in helping me learn the lessons revealed in this book. Not only through their direct actions, but also by the way they interacted with my grandparents (and vice-versa). They've served – and continue to serve – as wonderful role models to me, my brother and sisters, and my entire generation of cousins.

Much thanks goes to Kenny's wife Betsy and my wife Betsy (yes, they're both named "Betsy") who scanned the book for typos and other such annoying phenomena. My daughter Cesidia provided yeoman's service as my publicist, securing radio and TV interviews before the book was even published. My daughter Catarina begged me to have her do the cover. She did a wonderful job with it. Finally, my son Peter did me the courtesy of being my joke tester. If he laughed at my jokes, I included thing in this book. (Reader be Warning, I took the liberty of including some he didn't laugh at.)

I'd also like to thank the officials of the Erie County Fair, who have been very kind to me (and my family) through the years. Not only have they graciously acknowledged my family's legacy at the Fair (by honoring both my grandfather and his namesake son, who runs Salvatore's Pizza Trailer today), but they've also allowed me to sign my books during the annual event.

Alas, I wish I could turn back the clock and go back to the era of which I write within these pages, but, if there's one thing my grandparents insisted on, it's that we always look towards the future and never dwell in the past. What they never told me, and what I wish I could thank them for today, is that one can build one's future success only on the solid foundation of one's past. My grandparents provided some very key building blocks to that foundation.

And that's why I wrote this book.

PROLOGUE: A CHRISTMAS CAROL

(December, 1970)

ett' e mezz'!" roared my grandfather as he rose from his seat. He towered over my meek ten-year old body like a grizzly bear rearing above its prey.

I saw hunger in his ferocious eyes. But I wasn't afraid. I knew the next lesson was about to begin.

"Sam!" yelled my grandmother, instinctively and in that terse disapproving way it seemed she could summon up from nowhere. Immediately the aggressiveness vanished from my grandfather's countenance and he obediently shrank back into his chair.

"What do you want me to do, Flo? Those are the rules," he said, timidly trying to justify his actions. Sensing his own reticence, he tried to counter it by continuing with a voice rising in intensity and ending with a tone of self-assured purpose. "He dealt me the King of Diamonds. The rule is you have to let the dealer know as soon as you get it. You're *supposed* to shout '*Sette e la mezza*,' too. Do you expect me to treat him any different than anyone else? Sooner or later he's gonna go out in the real world. You think they're gonna treat him nice? No. Look at him. If he doesn't toughen up, they're gonna eat him alive."

"But he doesn't know Italian," countered my grandmother, this time much calmer.

"He's smart enough to learn," answered my grandfather, a tinge of mocking anger in his tenor.

"That's OK, Grandma," I interrupted, staving off one of those traditional Christmas Eve family arguments Hollywood demands of its Italian characters. "I get it. He's just following the rules." So ended, on the initial card of the initial hand, my first ever chance to act as dealer in our family's annual card game.

The truth was, my grandfather never wanted me in the game in the first place. The card game is called "Seven and a Half" (or *Sette e la Mezza* in Italian). It's just like Twenty-One, except picture cards are worth a half instead of ten and the objective is to get your cards to add up to seven and a half. It's generally played on Christmas Eve, but we played it throughout the Holiday season. It's an old game (some call it a predecessor of Blackjack) and it has some variations. One of them includes choosing a wild card – usually the King of Diamonds – that, in our case, made you an instant winner. If you were dealt the King of Diamonds, or if you were dealt a "natural" (i.e., two-card) seven and a half and the dealer didn't equal you, you immediately took over as dealer.

15

Oh, I forgot to mention a very important thing. Seven and a Half is a betting game. Being dealer makes it a whole lot easier to win money. It's good to be the dealer. You want to be the dealer. So, when I finally won the right to deal I was very excited and everyone saw that. When I lost the deal on the first card, well, you can imagine how sympathetic all the adults were.

Except for my grandfather.

You see, he loved playing the game. He loved the betting. He liked winning the money, but there was something he enjoyed even more. As with many a passionate Sicilian, he was prone to dramatic outbursts like the one just mentioned. This tended to make his poker face about as effective at hiding things as a see-through dress. If his emotions betrayed him so much, why did he relish the game? More than winning a pot full of chips, he liked winning the psychological battle even more. If my grandfather were to have ever appeared on Jeopardy, he would have vigorously bet it all on the final round. His only purpose in this maneuver would have been to capture the reaction of, and surprise, his competitors. Sometimes that alone – not a shrewd poker face – was enough to win the round.

Ironically, my grandmother had better command of her emotions. She could be cool and calculating if she needed to be. When the situation demanded, she could be a loud aggressor (and that meant using tough – but never R-Rated – words). And she could turn it off and on without batting an eyelash. She had the perfect poker face. Except, she rarely won. Why? Unlike my grandfather, (and more like her depression-era generation) she was more prone not to take risks. They were a perfect couple.

Anyway, for my grandfather, having a kid – and one not yet even a teenager – in the game cheapened this challenge. These Christmas Eve games generally included adults of his generation (it was, after all, an Italian Christmas Eve, and that meant a lot of people with nothing to do except wait for Midnight Mass). They allowed my father and my older uncles to play, but that was about it.

I didn't know it at the time. In fact, back then I thought everyone loved to count and add (and all that math-numbers kinda stuff) as much as I did. Sure, I did well at those speed tests in school, but, then again, I don't ever remember being the fastest, and I do remember finishing behind a lot of kids. My parents and my grandparents knew I was good at math before I did. They also knew I liked watching them play Seven and a Half. One year, my father let me and my brother Kenny partner with him. Each of us sitting on a respective knee, he'd let us make decisions and overrule them if we made the same the mistake twice. That's when my grandfather started letting his displeasure be known.

"Pat," he'd growl whenever my brother and I took a little too long to make a decision, "you gonna play or are you gonna let your kids run your life?"

My father ignored him. He wasn't being disrespectful, though. After all, this was my mother's father, not his. Had his own father, sitting two seats over, seconded this complaint, my brother and I would have been sent off to the family room to watch whatever was on TV. Instead, my paternal grandfather was too busy trying to count the cards to see if he should take another card or not. He didn't have time to pay attention to what his counterpart was saying. Sensing this as approval, my father let us continue to play.

I don't know how I learned to play so fast. My parents and grandparents liked to think it was some innate thing (having to do with my fondness for math). At first I did too. Then, as I got better and better, I realized it wasn't something pre-programmed in my genes. Additionally, I didn't know the concept of counting cards, let alone how to count them. My seemingly "natural" decision-making process really represented the sum of watching the adults play over and over again. I noticed certain patterns, not in the cards, which, by definition, were random, but in the players – patterns of betting, of asking for more cards, and of folding.

Most of all, I learned winning meant understanding the psychology of the players more than the arbitrary order of appearance of the cards. The cards actually did mean something. It's just, other than deciding whether or not to take another card, you couldn't really do anything about it. It was all up to chance.

You could, on the other hand, read the faces of the players. And that meant you might be able to make a reasonable guess as to what they're betting on. And that was really important if you were the dealer. And that's because only the dealer plays against everyone. And that's why the dealer can make a lot of money. And that's why you want to be the dealer.

And that's why, several hands after our opening scene, when my grandfather dealt me the King of Diamonds, I jumped up from my chair (yes, all five feet of mini-me) and shouted *Sett' e Mezz'!*

The whole table burst out laughing, but the loudest was my grandfather. He looked at me with that silent twinkle in his eye. I might have been ten years old, his gaze told me, but I had learned my lesson.

I could sense he wanted to teach me more. Much more.

PART I

A Day In the Life of a Carny

– More Than Bending Steel with Bare Hands –

1: WAKE-UP CALL

My eyes peek open from under the cool refreshing bed sheet. Behind the undulating softness of the pillow sits the alarm clock. I never figured out how to set the alarm. I don't need to. The subtle yet discernable noise of clanking cups and rattling utensils from my grandparents' kitchen down the hall make sure my brother and I get up. And if it isn't this audio bustle, then the thick aroma of brewed coffee, the frank fragrance of freshly burnt toast, and the sweet smell of newly-lit cigarettes would certainly wake us.

The silent alarm clock tells me it's six o'clock in the morning. "Barely four hours of sleep," I sigh after quickly doing the math. I turn over to see my unmoving brother on the next bed.

"Kenny, you awake?" A bit of grunt comes from his body.

"C'mon, Kenny," I nag him. "It's time to get up. We're already late. Don't make Grandma and Grandpa holler at us."

He still doesn't move. And this time he doesn't even bother grunting.

Well, I don't want to get in trouble, so I get up.

The next few minutes are a blur. There's barely time for a shower and a shave. And shaving is important to me. I don't want even a few days growth of beard to hide the faux-Fu Manchu mustache I've been cultivating since the middle of hockey season last winter.

Somehow, we manage to find ourselves sitting in the back seat of a hulking Oldsmobile drenching in a sea of stale nicotine. Kenny's still sleeping, only now he's fully dressed – well about as fully as you want to be dressed for a hot summer day in Western New York. I'm still deciding whether to cheat the day and catch a few last minutes z's. I decide it's more interesting to pay attention to what's going on in the front seat.

My grandfather's driving, the omnipresent cigarette stuck between his lips. Wisps of smoke gently curl from its tip before disbursing to join their invisible brethren forever haunting the interior of this Detroit tank. Next to him, my grandmother, her head barely visible above the seat, recites a list of today's order of battle. I can't tell if she's reading it from a piece of paper or whether she's got it memorized. She probably has it memorized. After all, she's been doing this non-stop for more than twenty years. I also can't tell if she's trying to tell this to my grandfather or if she's just repeating it for her own good. In either case, my grandfather isn't paying attention. He's probably running through a to-do list in his own mind.

"Flo, did we remember the passes?" he abruptly says, as if breaking from a trance. (Don't forget. He's driving.)

My grandmother quickly fumbles through her purse. "Yeah, I got 'em."

In all the years working there, I could never quite get this. Here we are, vendors at the Fair. I'm guessing we had to pay the Fair something to be a vendor. If that's the case, then why do we still need parking passes and admission passes? Doesn't the Fair already know why we're coming? After all, we're part of the show, we're part of the reason people come to the Fair. You'd think they'd at least remember us.

Of course, if I'd had just paid more attention, I would have seen that each morning we come, the people at the gate aren't necessarily the same. The new ones won't know us from Adam. That's why we need the passes. We turn right onto Quimby Road. I can see Gate Two on the other side of the vast grassy field that will soon house the parked cars of thousands of eager Fairgoers. We turn into the parking lot and head towards the gate. Will today be the day those passes prove critical. My stomach twists. It's like crossing the border into Canada. There never should be a problem. We do it all the time. But there's always this chance some "i" isn't dotted or some "t" isn't crossed. And, if we happen to run into an unforgiving guard,… Well, let's just say I've heard stories that can make your stomach twist.

That's why my stomach is twisting right now.

2. MORNING RITUAL

Today's actually a lucky day. The people at the gate are old timers. They cheerfully greet my grandparents and spend a few moments exchanging pleasantries. This amiability pays off. We're carrying supplies for the stand and we're here early enough where the guard lets us drive the car right to the pizza stand.

This is good. The alternative would have been parking in the parking lot and carrying those boxes up the incline of the Avenue of Flags. It's not that steep, but it's steep enough to notice. And, of course, you can guess who would have gotten stuck carrying those boxes, right? Me and my brother. I smile at the friendly guard, relieved he just saved me and Kenny a lot of work. Kenny would be relieved, too, but he's still sleeping.

Our stand is a short left turn from the top of the Avenue of Flags. It's across from the main entrance of the grandstand. The car crinkles on the loose gravel before rolling to a stop in front of the stand. I gently ooze out of the cavernous back seat, ready to begin the day. Kenny is not only wide awake, but he's already one step ahead of me. He's carrying all the boxes to the back of the stand before I can even close the door on my side of the car. I look around. The long shadows hide the morning sun, keeping us in a grayish dim. I can see a few loose papers blow through the empty lane, like some casual tumbleweed rolling through a ghost town. We're the first vendors in our section today. Although we're alone, it's not as scary as closing at night. I figure all the bad folks are still sleeping.

My grandfather unlocks the padlocked door in the back of the stand and lets my grandmother, Kenny and me in. My grandmother places her purse under the counter and leaves. She's got to run an errand and my grandfather has to go park the car. It's up to me and Kenny to prep the stand for opening.

23

That's how much our grandparents trust us. We've been doing it for several years now. For them, except during the daily rushes and dealing with various officials, the Fair has become a time to socialize.

Strike that. I should say, by delegating the mundane duties to me and my brother, my grandparents have the opportunity to sell the product in ways they are far better at than me or Kenny. At first we thought they were just spending all that time talking with old friends – many who they just see once a year at the Fair. We're old enough now that we know they aren't just chatting away with friends, they're extending their good will with loyal customers who regularly return. Knowing that somehow gives me a good feeling, like I've learned an important lesson. Who knows?

Along these lines, this is the time of day when my grandfather would ask us to make a whole pie or two for him. He would then give these away for free to certain people. Sometimes I think he's being bullied into giving away free pizza. Today's a little different, though. Today he asks us to make a pizza for him and put it in a box. We know he'll be bringing it down to the good folks at Gate 2 as a thank you for letting us drive to the stand this morning. That's a good reason to give away a free pizza.

One of the first things my grandfather taught us in how to prep the stand for opening was to not open the front until we're ready to serve. We found this out the hard way once. The front consisted of a continuous counter with two plywood shutters hinged at the top. There was a mechanism to lock these closed for the night. After undoing that, it was a simple matter of swinging the plywood up and hooking the loose end to the ceiling. This floods the stand with the morning light, making it much easier to see inside the stand.

Well, we did this once before we were ready. Believe it or not, as soon as we opened the shutters, people would come and ask if we had any pizza to sell. And the ovens weren't even turned on yet! As I said, we did this once before we were ready. Only once.

Mistake made. Lesson learned. It never happened again.

Prepping means cleaning the front of the stand, getting all the supplies out, readying the first pizza, but, most importantly, it means turning on the oven. We have a huge pizza oven. I think it can cook eight pizzas at once. I'm not sure. Kenny's the cook. I'm the guy in front. They put me in front because they thought I could add quickly and not make many mistakes. It turns out I can do a lot of other "front" things, too, but that's for later in the day. Anyway, being able to cook something like eight pizzas all at once is important during the daily rushes. It takes 10 minutes to cook a pizza. (Again, I'm not sure. If you really want to know, ask Kenny.) In a rush, we can easily sell eight pizzas in that amount of time. Us guys in the front, we don't like waiting. It's the responsibility of the guys in the back – the ones cooking the pizza – to make sure we (and, therefore, the customers) aren't waiting.

Which brings us to the first important decision of the day…

3: SOFT OPENING AND MORNING BREAK

When do we put in the first pizza? Our grandparents are away from the stand most of the early morning doing what they do best. It's up to me and Kenny to decide when to actually open. My grandmother left just enough money to seed the till (they trust us, but they're not stupid – two young boys, barely out of their teenage years – can easily be overcome by a gang looking for easy money).

We have to wait for the oven to get hot enough to cook the pizza. When it does, we decide to pull the trigger. We initiate the opening process. Kenny puts the pizza in and, when he tells me it's half-way done, I lift the shutters. Light pours into the stand and Salvator's Pizza is open for a new day.

Despite what I said before about people rushing to buy pizza as soon as the shutters open, that doesn't always happen. In fact, it doesn't usually happen. What happens is we make a couple of quick sales. We won't make another pizza until we're down to two slices. This is a particularly slow morning and the pizza sits out for a while. In this business, if the product doesn't look like it's fresh out of the oven, it doesn't woo the customer like it should. With about half the pizza unsold, these slices soon look like they're not fresh out of the oven.

There's only one thing to do. Kenny puts the next pizza in, hoping we can sell the old slices before the new pizza is done. I suggest an alternative.

"These slices are looking old," I tell my brother. "We need to get rid of them before the new pizza comes out. Why don't we do this: Since we didn't have breakfast, let's eat the old slices if we don't sell them."

"Sounds good to me," says Kenny, who immediately grabs one of the slices and starts chomping on it.

Well if he's eating one, then I'm going to eat one, too. And so I do. Long before the next pizza is ready. It's a breakfast our mother wouldn't be proud of, but we're hungry and this is good pizza. We finish our breakfast and sell a few more slices by the time our grandparents get back. They're ready to take over, allowing Kenny and me to take a break.

Now, what shall we do today? The pre-lunch break, for me, consists of walking around as much of the Fair as possible. It's still early and not all the attractions are open, but enough are so I can begin to spec out the day's quarry. What do I want to get today? Who has something worth trading for? Where's the best sales pitch happening? These are the questions whose answers I seek and I walk fast to cover as much ground as possible. Sometimes I go with Kenny, sometimes we go our separate ways. Today we do the latter. I have no idea where he's going.

I begin by walking towards the top of the Avenue of Flags. WBEN radio has their live remote just past the wooden sausage stand next to us. It was from these speakers that I learned of Groucho Marx's death one hot August afternoon a few years earlier. Today I take a casual glance at the disc jockey, half hoping he'll ask me to appear on the air, half keeping a professional "who-cares" demeanor. (I've got my own AM show in New Haven, and when you're in the business and you encounter your more famous counterparts, you're supposed to act cool, not like some naïve groupie.)

Soon I'm walking briskly around the grandstand, ignoring the carnival barkers egging me on to play their games – they demonstrate just how easy it is to sink a basketball into a rim barely bigger than the ball's diameter. When I'm feeling like a carny, I talk shop with them. Today I'm on a mission.

I slow to hear the hypnotic voice of the I-Got-It caller. The smooth baritone drones "Aaaallll, ready now. Ball Number One…" I dream of someday winning. They don't really have any prizes worth winning (for me, at least), it's just the game looks cool. It's you against a large tic-tac-toe matrix of squares, and you're armed with an unlimited supply of little red balls. These balls seem to have a mind of their own. Not only do I see people aiming for one corner square and the ball bouncing to the opposite corner, they also have a tendency to escape their confines. You can travel almost anywhere on the Fair grounds and you're sure to see at least two or three little red I-Got-It balls strewn on the grass, gravel, or even rolling on the occasional blacktop.

At the Bazaar Building, I go straight to the Dairy Farmer's milk stand. I select a blue pen, fill my name out on the entry form for the raffle and stuff the pen in my pocket. I do this twice a day. It gets me enough pens to use for my entire college career, (and beyond). The pens are free by the way, I'm not stealing them Next it's the Encyclopedia Britannica salesman. I listen as he pitches several interested prospects. I dream of owning those books, but know I can't afford them.

A quick peek at my watch tells me I've got to head back before the lunch rush. I dart out of the Bazaar Building in full power-walk mode. The morning break is over.

4. HIGH NOON AT THE ERIE COUNTY FAIR

I get back to the stand in plenty of time to get ready for the lunch-time rush. Kenny's already there, getting the pizzas ready for the oven. They're not in yet, but he's making sure they're ready when the time comes. While my grandfather's not looking, he grabs a piece of pepperoni from the bag and eats it. He's really biding time until I'm at my proper station.

I have to admit. The day starts slow and it takes a while to really wake up, but, by the time the lunch-time rush arrives, my body is pumped with adrenaline. Same with Kenny. It drives us to prepare for the coming hoard. We plot out our pizza making strategy, get the first few in the oven, and wait. I even bark out a few lines at the passing crowd like you'd expect from any Carny. (Incidentally, carnival barking is a great way to develop speaking from your diaphragm.)

We're all in our positions. I'm in the front ready to serve. Kenny's in the back ready to cook, Grandpa standing right next to him. Grandma's in her lounge chair just outside of the door in the rear of the stand. She's sitting in the shade while I'm standing in the baking hot sun. She's poised to jump to the front of the stand when the lunchtime rush hits. I'm making sure the bright sun illuminates me for the crowd.

It's a little trick I learned when I saw a picture my father took of me and Kenny standing in the front of the stand. The back of the stand is dark and, if no one is standing in the front, the stand looks black and empty. When I stand in the front, though, and the full intensity of the noon-time sun bathes me in light, the contrast between my glowing figure against the dark background is enough to catch peoples' eyes. And the first part of getting someone to buy pizza is to look them right in the eye.

Alas, when will we ever learn? There's never a lunch-time rush. The Fair is a nocturnal phenomenon. People tend to come later in the day, after work.

Those that come around lunch-time have usually had lunch at home, preferring to spend their money on the rides and games at the Fair, not the food. My grandmother is sitting in the shade behind the stand, but in a position to watch over us. My grandfather is hidden in the back making sauce. The customers have disappeared and, once again, we have pizza getting cold on the front counter. So Kenny and I eat the leftover slices for lunch.

Just then my grandfather comes in to put the sauce into the refrigerator. Kenny and I both have mouthfuls of pizza. My grandfather shakes his head. "You two guys, I don't know what to do with you. You're eating all the profits."

By the afternoon, the mid-summer heat reaches full intensity. This is one of the downsides of working in the front of the stand – you have to stay out in the sun all day. When it's this hot, it's tough to sell hot pizza, but it's easy to sell cold Pepsi. I have become an expert at determining when the canister of Pepsi needs to be replaced and Kenny has become an expert at unhooking and rehooking the troublesome connections to said canisters. Here's the thing about Pepsi – they have an exclusive deal with the Fair. Coke tried to sneak in on Pepsi's turf one year by providing red uniforms with the Coke logo to the Fair's official marching band. Pepsi quickly put a stop to that. Pepsi supplies all the stands. By the way, you're only allowed to sell pop in official Fair cups. This helps the Fair monitor vendor says. The trouble is, you have to buy these cups., and that adds to the expenses.

When my grandmother learned this, she complained. Thirsty workers need to wet their whistle. These weren't sales, but if we were forced to use official Fair cups, these would be counted as sales. Her argument convinced, the powers that be to give her "no-charge" cups so workers could drink without getting charged. She soon started to bring her own no-charge cups. On hot afternoons like today, I'd take full advantage of those no charge cups. Standing in that hot sun, I gulp down the icy pop, trying to make drinking a Pepsi look as refreshing as possible. Every once in a while, I catch someone's eye and they amble over for a cool one.

Those aren't the only eyes I catch. You know how I told about the disadvantages of standing in the front on a sizzling day? And remember how I implied "fully" dressed wasn't as "full" as you would think when the thermometer soars? Well the sum of that equals one of the advantages of spending your youth in the front of the stand. And today is no different, as dozens of pretty girls with no desire to showcase an expansive wardrobe pass by. In true nerdy fashion, I proudly admit, "a few even talked to me."

But that's it. The reality is I'm a carny. And their mothers would disapprove.

Of course, it's not only young girls, it's old ladies, too. They'd come up and talk to me, usually to ask if my grandparents were around. Today, though, with one eye trying to woo customers and the other trawling for halter tops, an old lady – old enough to be my grandparents' parent – comes up and asks, "Are you Lena's son?"

Well, "Lena" being my mother's name, I instinctively answer "Yes."

This old lady gets really excited and starts babbling something in Italian to her old lady friends around her. She then starts talking to me. She smiles as if I were an old friend and chats away like a long-lost cousin. I have no clue who she is, but smile and laugh politely at her stories. By the way, she's telling her stories in alternating lines of English (I understood most of that part) and Italian (I only understood one or two words). So, I have no idea who this lady is, I have no idea what she is saying, but I act in an engaged and respectful manner, as if I'm fully aware of everything.

Soon, the entire gaggle of old ladies behind this old lady, perhaps noticing what a nice young man I am, huddle around us. It now appears as if the first old lady, by virtue of her now confirmed friendship with "Lena," has become a bit of a celebrity among her cohorts. They want a piece of the action, too.

It's too much for me to handle. The corner of my eye catches a glimpse of my grandmother, seated in a lounge chair in the threshold of the rear doorway. She's trying to keep from laughing.

"Grandma!" I motion to her, waving my hands as if to say, "Come and rescue me."

She does. She doesn't come through the stand, though. She walks around to the front, introduces herself as "Lena's son's wife" and draws the women away from me and away from the front of the stand. This clears valuable counter space for real customers.

It soon becomes obvious she's not referring to the Lena who's *my* mother, she's referring to the Lena who's my *grandfather's* mother. (Yes, in keeping with Italian tradition – although there were other reasons – my mother was named after her.) I signal for my grandmother to come up to the front. She bails me out of this crazy mess, and I go back to girl-watching.

The lull of the afternoon brings out our marketing tricks. I've taken the cue from my grandfather and I pull out his over-sized sunglasses, my own silly hats, and start barking. Sometimes I shout tried and true slogans like, "Pizza, it's nutritious and delicious!" Other times I'll randomly eyeball an innocent passerby – or, more effectively, his girlfriend – and ask directly for the sale. Yet other times I will randomly start singing popular tunes with made-up words. Today I do the latter, as I'm in the mood to adlib… ("….simply because I'm adlibby" – can you name that tune?).

Soon, it's apparent we're about to enter the after-lunch lull. This means only one thing. It's time for our last break of the day.

5. AFTERNOON DELIGHT

I t's time for the afternoon break and this time my brother and I decide to begin the venture together. He wants to show me a video game. "Chris, let's play this game I found," my grandfather overhears him say. Well, you should see how fast my grandfather's forehead goes from nothing to angry!

"How many times have I told you not to play those games!" he yells. "They're crooked. They'll steal your money."

"But Grandpa," I say, "these aren't carnival games with prizes, these are video games we play for fun."

"That's even worse," he bellows in a tone that says no logic will change his mind. "Those things will steal your money – and you don't even have a chance to get a prize." He pauses, and seeing we are going to go regardless of what he says, he harrumphs, "Go ahead! Waste your money! What do I care."

We go, but the game – a female version of Pac-Man? It'll never work – excites me much less than my brother, and we're soon on our separate ways again. I'm off to make a trade. I'm eyeing a particularly fine trinket being given away as a promotion. I know my grandfather has already hollered at me several times for trading his pizza. But, I see *him* giving it away, so why can't *I* do the same only get something in return? Still, I don't make a big deal about it so he never knows about *this* trade. One of these days, though, I'll surprise him and show him I can trade just as good as he can.

This afternoon calm doesn't affect just us. The entire Fair seems to take a break after lunch. Hmm, come to think of it, it's like lunch is just a quick practice for the rest of the day. It's like those pre-game drills. You come out of the locker room and run through a few simple plays on the field. Then you go back into the locker room until game time.

Only, we have no locker room at the Fair. And when I say we, I don't just mean me and my brother, I mean all the carnies. Many, like my grandparents, stand near their stands in the shadiest place possible. A few, like Kenny, have a chance to go exploring. Fewer yet seize upon this down time to trade.

Understand this: There are two kinds of traders. There's the big-time traders (like my grandfather). They own their businesses and they can make some really intense trades. My grandfather didn't just give away free pizza in exchange for some future favor, he actively traded pizza outright. He would trade pizza for show tickets (that I never saw him use – he'd usually get them for friends and family). The biggest trade I saw him make was getting Andy Williams tickets for my parents, but I'm sure he had bigger trades.

Anyway, those were the big-time traders. Then there were the rinky-dink traders. That's where I fit in. I really didn't have much of my own to trade. I had a very limited supply of pizza (that I would often take from my "lunch" allotment – yes, that means I'd trade the slices I was supposed to eat for lunch; thus, skipping that meal altogether). There's so much free stuff at the Fair it's hard to trade. You need to get your hands on something that cost money. At the Fair, food costs money. Pizza is food. Pizza is money.

The downtime in the afternoon was the best time to trade. People were both awake and had taken their day's inventory. Sometimes, all you could do during the lull is make a preliminary deal, then hope your trading partner ends up with excess inventory by late in the day so the deal could be consummated. A lot of times I'm not really in the market to trade, I'm just actively getting bids and asks. Today is one of those days. I have to be careful, though. If someone thinks I'm just window shopping, they might rebuff any effort I make to deal with them. Trading is not as easy as it seems. It takes a lot of thinking and a lot of being friendly with people.

My brother doesn't like to trade. To be honest, I don't know if Kenny really doesn't like to trade, or if he really just doesn't like to get hollered at by my grandfather. Maybe he figures we each have our own things our grandfather hollers at us about. He'll leave me the one about getting hollered at for trading. He'll take the one about getting hollered at for eating the food. I guess it's worth it to him. It doesn't involve anyone else and he gets some food out of it. In either case, Kenny doesn't trade. What he does do is find all the free stuff. Then he gets as much of it as possible. Sometimes he finds something really cool, but it costs money. Then he tries to get me to buy it.

Today he comes back with a bag of free things he got at the 4H Building and the new dome behind us. Actually, he comes back with four bags, one for him, one for me and one for each of our grandparents. My grandfather looks at it disapprovingly. "Why'd you get all this junk," is all he'll say. My grandmother, on the other hand, says, "Thank you, Kenny. That was very thoughtful of you." She also gives my grandfather one of her patented evil-eye stares.

We notice the sun has begun its descent. The late afternoon falls upon us. My aunt and uncles are getting off from work and, one by one, they begin to show up at the pizza stand. This is the pre-pre-dinner rush. The dinner rush is a real rush, so this is an important part of the day. We never know who's going to be there, so my grandmother waits until now to make the final assignments. Today I get assigned to the front with my aunt and grandmother. My brother is at his usual place by the oven, with my grandfather and one of my uncles. My other uncle will switch between the front and the back as needed.

There's one more thing we have to do during the pre-pre-dinner rush – we have to eat dinner. There will be no time to eat dinner during the dinner rush and, making matters worse, we don't know when the dinner rush will end. Sometimes it can go all the way to closing. In addition, we can't really predict when it will start. Sometimes it starts before we think it should start, during the pre-dinner rush. So we eat dinner during the pre-pre-dinner rush.

We usually eat pizza, but today is a special day. One day during the Fair we get Chivetta's Chicken – and today would be that day! I've never been able to figure out the pattern in determining which day is the Chivetta's Chicken day. I'm thinking my grandmother picked today because Kenny accidentally let it slip out we had pizza for breakfast in addition to the pizza she knew we ate for lunch. Anyway, Chivetta's never disappoints. We eat it. Now we're ready.

It's a good thing we ate early, because the dinner rush today starts during the pre-dinner rush time. It doesn't seem like a rush, but experience tells me it is. It seems more like a lunch rush – steady, but manageable. But I can read the crowd and the crowd seems to be saying two things very clearly: 1) We're hungry; and, 2) We want pizza. In almost no time, the leisurely paced pre-dinner rush morphs into the madcap of a pure, unadulterated dinner rush.

5½. THE DREADED DINNER RUSH

Sorry. I'm in the middle of the dinner rush. No time to think, let alone talk. The lines in front of the stand stretch as far as I can see. Inside the stand it's pure pandemonium. People are shouting. Pizzas – whole pies and slices – are flying from the oven out into the crowd. Money is changing hands. There's no need for marketing gimmicks, silly sunglasses, or funny songs. You don't need to promote the product when it's going out the door faster than you can make it.

6½. THE EVENING GLIDE

The dinner rush lasts well into the post-dinner rush. And then, all of the sudden, it stops. We don't know why. We don't know when. We don't know where. None of us do. Not me. Not my brother. Not my uncles or aunt. Not my grandmother. But my grandfather knows. It's as if he's developed a sixth sense. My grandfather can always perceive when the rush will die just before it does. He knows, without fail, precisely when we'll enter the evening inter-regnum. He stops making pizzas, he stops cooking pizzas, all well in advance of the end of the rush. By the time the rush is over, we have very few slices left.

The evening inter-regnum gives us all a chance to rest. It gives my grandfather a chance to reassess the remaining inventory. He discovers we're short on dough (as in the stuff that makes the pizza crust, not the stuff we get paid for selling the pizza crust and its toppings). He goes to another pizza stand and gets more. You see, the various pizza stands for the most part cooperate. Late at night, the stands with extra supplies will often "lend" those supplies to the stands that are short on supplies. This is the Erie County Fair. It's a family friendly Fair and we're all part of the same family. Cut-throat competition is frowned upon.

It's not like we'll be making a lot of pizzas. From this point on, it's not unusual to sell only a couple more pies worth of pizzas. The added inventory is more of an insurance policy in two ways. First, if we get an unexpected rush, we're ready. Second, we'll need that inventory to start the next day. Suppliers deliver everything in the morning – but there are no guarantees as to exactly when they'll deliver. It's always safe to have enough supplies to make a half dozen pizzas in the morning – just in case the suppliers show up late or show up only to tell you they're out of what we're looking for.

The evening pause sometimes gives my aunt and uncles a chance to leave, but they usually stay until after the post-fireworks rush. That's what they do tonight, and it's a good thing. Like the dinner rush, the post-fireworks rush is intense. It helps that we're located directly across from the main entrance (and, in this case, exit) to the grandstand. As the people pour out of the racetrack, it seems like they all make a bee line for our stand. Again, the lines are long. It's a good thing my grandfather got that extra dough.

But, like all post-fireworks rushes, this one is over quickly. Oh, we'll still get a few stragglers, but I can tell we've cooked our last pizza for the day. As if to emphasize the point, my grandfather turns off the oven and the hot stand finally has a chance to cool. Outside the stand, Fairgoers, eager to call it a day and go home, finally go home.

Not us. The long closing is often the busiest – and most dangerous – time of the day.

7½. DAY IS DONE

As the crowd begins to thin out, and as my aunt and uncles leave before us, we begin to appreciate the old "safety in numbers" adage. Soon, the only people left roaming the empty grounds are not the kind of people you want to be stuck in a dark alley with. And the alley is dark.

This is the beginning of seeing how grandpa's "free" gifts pay off. One of the places that he'll often give pizza to is the police barracks just three spaces down. Closing is a desolate time. There's not a lot of people around to help in case you get in trouble (remember, we're carrying all that cash we earned today). I'm very happy to realize the benefits of Pay Off #1: Getting in the good graces of the cops walking the beat where you live. My grandfather wasn't giving away a pizza for free when he gave it to the police. Just like the gatekeeper this morning, he was giving them a free pizza to thank them for their help – in case he ever needed their help.

Closing the stand can take up to a half hour. The first thing we do, save for turning off the oven, is to put the shutters down – but only after we wipe the front counter clean. I take care of cleaning the front of the stand with my grandmother. Kenny takes care of cleaning the back of the stand with my grandfather. At some point before we're done cleaning the front, my grandmother breaks away. She's silently taking care of the money, putting it all in a small satchel and gives it to my grandfather. One by one, as our jobs are complete, we exit through the rear of the stand. My grandfather is last and he locks the padlock on the door.

With the stand now closed, it's simply a matter of walking – or in the case of my grandfather, waddling – down the Avenue of Flags to the parking lot and our car. It's almost midnight. We've been here for about sixteen hours. Sitting on the soft seats in that smelly car will seem like heaven after this long

36

day. The only trouble – my grandparents walk so slow it'll take us forever to get there!

That's when Pay Off #2 hits. One of the Fair officials meets us at the top of the Avenue of Flags. He's driving a golf cart. It's big enough to fit all of us. He offers a ride to the gate. We graciously accept. On the way down, I hear the man tell my grandfather, "By the way, thanks for the pizza. The guys really liked it. Uh, how much do we owe you?"

"It's on the house," says my grandfather.

We leave the lights of Gate 2 and head into the large expanse of the dark parking lot. The downside of driving to the stand this morning is that all the close parking spaces were taken when my grandfather finally drove the car back to the parking lot. It's quite a distance from the gate.

Then something scary happens.

Some husky guy, obviously drunk, comes out of nowhere. He's built like a steel worker – large and foreboding. He shouts to my grandfather, "Sell a lot of that dago pizza today?"

My grandfather smiles and speaks gregariously. He acts as if this guy were an old friend. My brother and I share a glance. We get a sense of trouble and silently communicate "get ready" to each other. We know the guy is probably salivating at the thought of how much money my grandfather was carrying in that satchel he was holding ever so close. We might be a bit skinny, but we're taller than my grandparents – and this guy. We're prepared to do what is necessary.

For the moment, my grandfather's friendly disposition seems to mollify the situation, but then the drunkard gets aggressive. He goes on a tirade, his mouth erupting with profanities and more Italian slurs. This doesn't faze my grandfather, but my brother inches closer to the action. I notice my grandmother grab his hand as if she's afraid. Kenny instinctively positions himself between my grandmother and the action.

But then this guy's wife appears and starts yelling at him, telling him to back down and walk away. He does, and we silently – but swiftly – walk to the car.

Once we're safe and inside the car, my grandmother whips her head around to us in the backseat and sternly asks my brother, "Just what were you thinking?"

Kenny hems and haws, not saying exactly that he was going to make sure the drunken guy didn't steal the money. But definitely implying it. Not satisfied, my grandmother cuts him off and asks in terse tone, "Do you know what the most important thing to protect is?"

"Uh, the money?" answers my brother.

"No!" my grandmother snaps back. "You are."

Silence. We pause to reflect on what she just told us. But her genuinely caring concern removes whatever tension we had and we return to our normal end-of-day feeling, which is not what you might expect.

It's funny, but you'd think, by the end of a long hectic day like today, we'd be dead tired. No. The adrenaline rush that began before lunch has yet to subside within me and my brother. I think the same is true with my grandparents. We're in the car heading away from the Fair. You might believe we're heading home. No. We're going to a favorite all-night breakfast place of my grandparents. Every night, we come to this same place. Now you know why we didn't eat breakfast in the morning.

Finally, closer to two o'clock in the morning than my brain would like to think, we arrive home and I plop into bed. I don't remember taking my sweaty clothes off, but they are.

And now, to sleep. But instead of counting sheep, I hear my grandmother in the kitchen counting the money to make sure it reconciles with our sales records. I hear my grandfather spitting out inventory numbers so they could determine the number of pizzas sold that day. I never hear how that conversation ends as I am soon fast asleep.

To sleep. Perchance to dream.

But there's no time for that as my eyes peek open from under the cool refreshing bed sheet. The silent alarm clock tells me it's six o'clock in the morning. Time to wake-up and repeat.

PART II

PERSONAL VALUES

– Truth –

8. THE FOUR FUNDAMENTAL BASICS

On a pleasant summer day in June, 2013, I found myself in a third floor suite of the Affinia Manhattan Hotel on 7th Avenue smack dab between Penn Station and Madison Square Garden. I had been summoned there by the President and CEO of a large media firm. He wanted a chance to kick the tires before hiring me on as a consultant. For more than three years I had been writing for both digital and print properties under his company's banner.

He didn't want to talk to me about that. He was more interested in my own publications. Four years earlier, I started a small web-based news site from absolutely nothing. By the time I was eating eggs and bacon across the breakfast table from this business icon, the site had attained a well-regarded national reputation and had grown to thousands of subscribers. And that wasn't even my day job. What interested this media executive was how I accomplished so much in his target market while still maintaining a growing investment business.

I began by saying, "I guess I'm a serial entrepreneur…"

"More like a parallel entrepreneur!" interrupted the media chieftain.

I paused. His comment left me without words. I must have recovered, though, since his firm did hire me. But it made me rethink this entire "entrepreneurial" thing. Up until that point, I had always described myself as a serial entrepreneur. After all, I had started several businesses, some for me, some for other people. Looking back, I realized I had only actually sold one of them (and used the proceeds to start my current firm). In fact, this man who had never before met me (but certainly did his research on me) did a better job describing my business persona in his first sentence than I had my entire life.

Where did this persona come from? I've always considered myself an entrepreneur. I wasn't one of those "lemonade stand" kids, though. I aimed higher. In middle school I got my neighborhood friends to hold a carnival each summer. We'd invite kids from all the area neighborhoods to play games, watch movies, see wild west shows – you know, the usual sort of thing. And we charged a dime here, a dime there. One year, we actually grossed $21. (Hey, what can I say? I was a kid and, to me, that was a lot of money.)

I really shouldn't count that enterprise as a business though. All we saw was the revenue side of the ledger. Our parents took care of the expenses. They bought and developed the film we used to make our movies. They also bought the ingredients for (and cooked) the various cookies, cakes, and "mini-pizzas" we sold. Did we ever make money? Probably not. We'll never know. Our parents let us keep the revenue and never told us how much they spent.

Together with my brother, I started my first real business (a baseball card business) in high school. This wasn't merely bartering between friends. This was sharing space with adults at various hobby shows across the region. In college I started a polling/market research firm (and my brother started a sister firm at his college a year later). But I'll talk about these things much later on in the book..

So, is there a gene that carries the entrepreneurial trait, or is this something you pick up during the ordinary course of living? Looking back, it seems like it's innate – it's always been there. But, like my understanding of *Sette e la Mezza* described in the prologue, it's really less inborn and more learned. I can tell you one thing, though, it's not book learning. It's learning by doing, learning by living, learning by getting hollered at and learning by getting hugged.

You see, after several years of nearly two straight weeks of those twenty hours days described in the previous section, I had learned just about everything I needed to know about being an entrepreneur. I learned more about business than any two years of business school can teach you. I learned more about common sense and courtesy than any finishing school can teach you. In fact, I dare say I learned more about people than any 4-year degree in psychology or sociology can teach you.

All in all, everything I ever learned about how to succeed in business I learned by working in my grandparents' pizza stand at the Erie County Fair.

Operating a successful business means knowing more than just that specific business or even about business in general. It means knowing about all areas of life because they all play a role in making sure your business is one of those roughly three out of ten firms still operating ten years after they were started.

Yes this means possessing a good character. But good character alone does not lead to business success. I'll begin by listing the most basic of the basics. They're so basic they aren't mentioned in any of the various stories I relate in this book. Still, they permeate the roots of every story. I'll explain these four lessons and give a quick example of when they appear most obviously in the pizza stand. If you reread the next few paragraphs after reading the entire book, you may be able to see where these lessons pop up furtively in particular stories.

Lesson #1: You Need to be Organized – This applies both to your thinking and to your management skills as well as to the system under which your business operates. We see organization everywhere in the pizza stand, from the very beginning of storing, assembling, and disassembling the physical stand to the operating structure of the day. This daily structure includes the assignment of personnel duties and the management of product inventory, supplies, manufacturing (that's baking the pizza), and distribution (that's selling the pizza).

Lesson #2: You Need to have Guts – You've got to be brave enough to go against the current and to stand up against all those critics who complain about your going against the current. You don't see a whole lot of this in the pizza stand, but it does appear every once in a while. Where you'll really find this is in the backstory – the why and how decisions are made, including the very decision by my grandfather (at my mother's mean-spirited insistence) to close his grocery store – a steady cash business – and open a pizzeria – a relatively new idea at the time. People often say you need to have luck. That may or may not be true. I happen to think luck comes only after guts. My grandfather had the guts to take a chance on starting a pizza parlor when not many people had done it. Was he lucky that he started his pizza place just before it became a dining fad and preference that continues to this day? I say, without the guts, that "luck" would not have been there.

Lesson #3: You Need Persistence – Since when does everything always go as planned? It never does. There's a saying for this: Into each life a little rain must fall. There can be slow times during the day in the pizza stand. There can be slow days for the pizza stand. Indeed, there can be slow years for the pizza stand. Nothing inhibits selling pizza like a steady downpour. Our stand had no roof for the customers and, if it did, we'd likely only attract people trying to get out of the rain, not paying patrons. Yet, every hour of every day of every year, we were there. Heck, for a couple of years the Fair relocated the stand to a less traveled part of the grounds. This hurt business. Before the days of the internet and instant universal communications, our regulars had a hard time finding us. Did my grandparents pack up and leave? No. They stuck it out.

Lesson #4: You Need Discipline – It's one thing to say you're organized, to show you have guts and to demonstrate a little persistence, but it's another thing to actually do it. Discipline comes into play because you've got to demonstrate these three characteristics 24/7. Take one break from them and your business may never recover. People who don't appreciate what this means will complain of "the daily grind" or "being in a rut" or mindlessly doing the same things over and over again. It may sound like a cliché, but a successful business is like a well-oiled machine. It faithfully performs the same tasks *ad infinitum* in a reliable and predictable fashion. There was a time when pizza suppliers aggressively sold products that allowed pizza stands to make pizza faster. A lot of pizza stands bought into this. Not my grandfather. Though more efficient, these new products compromised his recipes. While you could provide the pizza to the customer faster, the pizza didn't taste as good. So, while pizza became a commodity at those other stands, our pizza still had (and still does have) that unique taste that kept (and keeps) people coming back year after year.

Before you start contemplating these four lessons too much, let's dive into the most important value you can have if you want to create a successful business that lasts through the generations.

9. FAMILY FIRST

In any story, you need to know the characters in order to best understand the plot. That's what this chapter is for. As a bonus, in introducing these characters, we'll reveal an underlying theme inherent in every pizza stand story. It's that family always comes first. It helps frame your life and it defines your life.

There are four main characters in this story: my mother's parents, my brother and me. My mother and her siblings, as well as my father's father, make some cameo appearances, but these stories revolve mostly around the four main characters. My brother and I, through our high school and college years, were called upon to fulfill our family obligation to help our grandparents with the pizza stand. Actually, this wasn't the burden it might sound like. In fact, we begged our parents to allow us to work at the Fair. We were, after all, full-fledged teenagers and the Hamburg Fair (as many of us native to the region still call it), was "The Show." It's the big-time. It's where everyone who's anyone wants to be. How could you not want to do this – no matter what your age?

I'm not kidding. Now pushing 54, I still get goose bumps when I'm invited to sign books at the Fair. If you want a sense of what I'm talking about – and a little history of the Fair itself – read the appendix at the end of the book. It's an excerpt from my book *50 Hidden Gems of Greater Western New York*. Titled "Back at the Old Pizza Stand," not only does it explain why the Erie County Fair is older than Erie County itself, but it also explains how my family came to be in the pizza business. It's a true story.

For a long time, my parents refused to allow us to work at the Fair. Yes, we were young, and they were afraid of something happening to us. The Erie County Fair – at the time the largest county fair in the nation and even bigger than the New York State Fair – had upwards to a million visitors (it has many more now and continues to be ranked among the largest county fairs in the nation). That's a lot of people for two little boys to get lost in. So the answer each year was, "No!"

To be honest, my grandparents didn't need the help. Still in their 50's, they could rely on my mother's younger brothers and sister to help. But by the mid-1970's my aunt and uncles had their own families and their own family responsibilities. The Fair was hard work. It really was twenty hour days for more than a week. As much as my grandparents appreciated the help from their children and as much as their children genuinely wanted to help their parents, my grandparents knew they couldn't be a ball and chain. They didn't want to hold back their own children from the joys of raising their own families.

As if timed to perfection, just as my aunt and uncles had to move on with their lives, my brother and I were big enough (and here I do mean physical stature) to work in the stand. We were told our grandparents needed our help and we were excited to provide it.

Because of our schedules, though, my mother and father stuck to one rule – we weren't allowed to help assemble or disassemble the stand. On the plus side, this might have saved us from experiencing lots of shouting and, at least in my mother's eyes, lots of dangerous power tools. I can't say for sure. I was never there. I was there, however, when things happened to the stand that required repair. So, yeah, I could see how things can proceed when you put a father and his sons together. That being said, it was no different than when my father worked on projects with his sons – except my brother and I didn't shout back. If we were lucky, though, we did get to use the electric drill.

Despite the usual, sometimes loud, uh, "conversational tone" one would expect from an Italian family, my grandfather undeniably trusted his children and was confident in their ability to do some things (emphasis on "some") much better than he could. When it came to fixing things in the stand, the only thing that might hold him back from calling my uncles to the rescue was the guilt he might have for bothering them. Of course, he never had an ounce of guilt if the matter was urgent.

Likewise, my aunt and uncles could be relied on to come in if needed, whether to fix equipment, repair the stand, or help out cooking or selling. Yes, there would often be raised voices, but when my grandfather made a decision, everyone listened and obeyed him. Except if my grandmother overruled him, then everyone – including my grandfather – listened and obeyed *her*. Likewise, when my aunt or uncles told Kenny or me what to do, if we didn't agree we complained. We didn't argue, we just suggested it was something we didn't think Grandma or Grandpa would do. Of course, if my aunt or uncles decided something in the absence of my grandparents, Kenny and I would listen and obey.

Yet, for all the loud voices that filled the air while they built that spindly stand made of flimsy angle irons and plywood, when push came to shove and the customers came pouring to the front of that same stand, the family operated its pizza making business like a well-tuned instrument. I've noticed this same trait in the many successful small businesses – and even some large ones – I've seen and worked with. Entrepreneurs work best (and their businesses survive longer) when they have a strong foundation. That foundation represents something they can always count on. It makes taking the risks necessary to succeed less daunting. It gives you an emotional safety net you can always fall back on. Yes, there are many successful businessmen whose businesses thrive into international renown who have forsaken their families, gone through serial trophy wives, and disowned their own children. Yet, I bet, when you look at the very beginning, when failure was most likely, they had a strong family behind them.

Lesson #5: The Family Always Comes First – The family comes before business. My grandparents would avoid calling up my aunt and uncles because they had their own young families to tend to and the pizza stand was never more important than the family. The family comes before pleasure. My brother and I always wanted to work at the pizza stand. It seemed like fun. And when we finally got the chance, we seized the opportunity and very rarely left the stand when it looked like things might get busy – except when our own parents came to the Fair. Despite our pleas to stay working in the stand, despite the need our grandparents appeared to have, they insisted we go experience the Fair with our parents. And so we did. Finally, the family comes before others. And that includes customers. Maybe you'll see why a little later.

Lesson #6: The Family has an Established Hierarchy – No one questioned my grandparents, and my grandmother usually let my grandfather call the shots. She knew he was the face of the franchise. She knew he made the sauce, and our tasty sauce is the one thing that made us stand out among all the other pizza stands. (Truth be told, my grandfather let us know both my grandmother and my great-great aunt Ziapepe were there in the pizzeria as he perfected the taste that he duplicated at the Fair. He also told us he'd often ask our mother – a professional home economist – for her expert opinion.) So my grandfather was in charge of everything about the business – the product development, the manufacturing of the product, and the marketing of the product. The one thing my grandmother made sure she controlled was the books. She had a natural math ability (despite never finishing high school). So we had this structure. And with structure comes order. And with order comes discipline. And with discipline comes success.

Lesson #7: The Family is the Meaning of Life – It makes us laugh. It makes us cry. It defines who we are. Ultimately, it is the source of true happiness. I suppose if I were a sociologist or an anthropologist I could explain why our species evolved this way, but I'm not. But I know what I see. The pizza stand is part of the Butera family legacy, and, more importantly, the Butera family legacy is forever imbued within the pizza stand.

Family may be the most important group you belong to, but it's not the only one. It's something we're taught if we ever played a sport. It's something we feel whenever we talk about our home town. It's something the best businesses try to emulate. And it's something I discuss in the next chapter.

10. IT'S AN HONOR MERELY TO BE A PART OF THE TEAM

Am I leaving out something? I mentioned the four characters. They're all important to my stories, but the most important character is "The Show" itself – the Erie County Fair. This wasn't some run-of-the-mill county fair. They are all Off-Broadway to the Fair's Broadway. Even the New York State Fair played second fiddle to the Erie County Fair. (At one point in its history, as you see in the appendix, State Fair officials actually came to the Erie County Fair to see how it was done.)

Before there were casinos in Western New York, if you wanted to see a genuine Vegas act, you had to go to the Erie County Fair. Sure it had tractor pulls and "the world's largest demolition derby" like those other fairs, but how many fairs could brag about hosting Joie Chitwood and the Hell Drivers? I'm not talking about one of his five touring groups, I'm talking about the man himself.

In a way, anyone who worked at the Fair could say they shared the stage with these celebrities. We're all part of the same show. This feeling permeates every single worker at the Fair, from the headliner to the lowly security guard. And I'm not throwing you some gratuitous platitude, I'm telling you the honest truth. Do you know how I know? I'll tell you. My father's father – Peter Carosa – was a security guard at the Erie County Fair. He was assigned to the Conservation Building, and each year he'd proudly serve. He might have been retired, but he still had a position of responsibility, and a public one at that!

I'm guessing you're probably asking, "Why does the Conservation Building need security?" and you might be on to something. The actual risk was likely much lower in the Conservation Building than in other parts of the Fair. No money changed hands. It attracted mainly young families. Most of the animals were stuffed; ergo, harmless. The only live animals could not survive outside their fish tanks. And, if trouble ever did occur, the Conservation Building was protected by two different forces. First, the police headquarters was located just up the street at the top of the Avenue of Flags. Second, several of the exhibiters in the Conservation Building were experienced outdoorsmen, hunting enthusiasts, or avid sportsmen. That meant they knew how to use guns and weren't afraid to demonstrate that particular expertise.

Despite these facts, Grandpa Peter still treated his job as critical to the success of the entire Fair. He showed up to work on time. He worked whenever he was asked. He knew the Conservation Building from stem to stern, and if someone stumped him with a question, he knew who to ask for the correct answer. He dressed professionally and his clothes were always neatly pressed (Grandma Gilda made sure of that).

In fact, nothing made him prouder than to wear the security guard uniform issued to him by the Fair officials. Each year, when it was time for the Fair, he made sure to model his uniform for all the family to see. And, out of respect, we always remembered the hours he worked at the Fair so we could be certain we saw him in action. Nothing made him prouder than to know his family came to see him working in full regalia in the Conservation Building.

Not only was he proud to strut his stuff for the family, but, in selecting him for this job, he knew the Fair officials bestowed upon him a lot of trust. And Grandpa Peter repaid the trust those officials placed in him. For the 4, 6 or 8 hours (however long a particular shift might be), he owned the building. He embraced his responsibility to protect all those inside his building – the exhibitors, the fairgoers, even his fellow security guards. Although it seemed more for show than for any real purpose (e.g., he was never issued a gun), he took the job seriously and performed his duties proudly.

The Fair wasn't just a job to him, he was part of its family. It's just like winning sports teams, the old neighborhood you had when you grew up, and the most successful businesses. Each of these organizations are effective because they've instill a culture that its members willingly identify with. It's sort of like patriotism. If listening to the National Anthem or hearing the phrase "truth, justice, and the American Way" makes your eyes swell up, then you know what I'm talking about. These are the lessons you'll want to emulate if you desire to have a prosperous business.

Lesson #8: Inspire Loyalty – You want every member of your organization to tell you "It's an honor to be invited to join the team." This is exactly the way Grandpa Peter felt about working at the Fair. It's the way I felt. It's the way my brother felt. I'm pretty sure it's the way my whole family felt. The loyal organization tells its members every job is the most important job. In turn, the loyal member doesn't just know his job, he knows everything about the business.

Lesson #9: Create an Atmosphere of Trust – Trust is earned and must be repaid when received. As an employer, extend trust whenever you hire a new employee. Employees return that trust by confirming it. They confirm the trust you placed in them by taking their job seriously and owning their responsibilities. An employer cannot ask for anything more.

Lesson #10: Develop and Promote a Culture of Tradition – If you're in a business that has uniforms, show employees how to wear them proudly by wearing them proudly. One of the first indications that a company is going south is when only half the employees wear the company colors. When you see your employees wearing their uniform proudly, you know you've already won half the battle. But that's not the only measure of tradition. You want everyone in the entire organization to know all the players and who best knows what. This will allow them to always protect and look out for the best interests of every constituency (or person) associated with the business (and if this doesn't bring up the idea of "great service" I don't know what will).

Putting family first and adopting a team-oriented attitude are all well and good. They're healthy, they're wise, and they're comfortable. But they lack zest. What do I mean by "zest"? Turn the page to find out.

11. LIVE LIFE TO THE FULLEST

I worked in my grandparent's pizza stand at the Erie County Fair from the beginning of high school through a year or so after I graduated from college. As you might imagine, school took up a sizable portion of my thinking capacity during that time. As caring parents, my success at school also took up a lot of my mother's and father's space of mind, too. They may have each had a different philosophy on how to approach such tasks, but they both agreed on one thing – getting the best grades were paramount to long-term success.

Now, grade-wise, life was easy in high school, and even the first couple years of college. In fact, it had gotten to the point where I just didn't believe grades meant anything. For example, at the close of the second semester my sophomore year, my math professor said I was right on the border-line between an A and a B. I told him to give me a B. My roommate, who witnessed the conversation, said on the walk back to our room, "You know, Chris, he would have given you an A if you would have asked him to."

"Yeah," I answered, "but grades don't matter."

By that time in my college career, I had fully scoped the joint out. I knew every nook and cranny that was important to me (grades not being one of them). More important, I had figured out how to connect the dots and get things – or do things – many people wanted but few knew how to obtain. It was a multi-step and somewhat iterative process. The first step was to get involved. The second step was to get to know people. The third step was to find out what people wanted. The fourth step was to figure out who had what they wanted. The fifth step was to find out what these new people wanted. And so on and so on until the loop could be closed and the dots were connected. Sometimes I had to short-circuit this loop, but that just meant I had to become a part of it.

So I got involved. With everything that interested me. And I made sure my level of activity was a very high one and very visible.

During one semester of particularly poor grades, my parents asked me if I was over-involved in extra-curricular activities. I answered, "No" only to discover it wasn't so much of a question as it was a criticism. I then proceeded to justify my actions.

"First," I said, "these activities are teaching me what I'm really going to need to know in life. Second, I'm like a shark. I've got to keep continually swimming. That's how I breathe. That's how I stay alive."

How did I know to answer this way? Well, I learned it by working in the pizza stand. At least for the first point. As far as I can recall, I brought up the second point because I had just watched some PBS documentary on sharks the night before. But that's not important.

What is important is learning how to smoothly and purposefully juggle activities. Multi-tasking, you see, isn't just a way of life; it's the way to success. It can increase your organizational value within a corporation. It can broaden your brand footprint if you're running your own business. Finally, it can lead to a fulfilling life where you help your neighbor and your neighbor helps you.

I'll break this down into two categories: the world inside the pizza stand; and, the world outside the pizza stand.

Sometimes, one man can run a pizza stand. Remember what I said about my grandparents leaving me and my brother to run things? One day, when we were all alone, Kenny took a particularly long morning break. During that break, we had a mini-rush. It was only me,… the customers,… the pizza oven,… the cash till,… and the genuinely proud desire to maintain the tradition of fine service and delicious pizza my grandparents spent the better part of their life building. Fortunately, my grandparents had trained both my brother and me in every facet of operating the pizza stand. Now, being the front man, I'm not saying it was easier for me, but I can't imagine my brother singing on-the-spot parodies and spouting one-liners to keep one group of waiting customers entertained at the same time I'm serving another group of customers. Oh, and did I mention I was doing these two things simultaneously with making change for a third set of customers?

You don't always want to be a Jack-of-all-trades, it's just that sometimes, if you want to succeed, you don't have a choice. The key is to juggle these tasks as effortlessly – and, in my case, as entertainingly – as an agile circus clown. Don't let the audience or the customers see you sweat, lest they begin to think the product or service they're buying may suffer from lack of quality. If you act like it only takes one person to run the stand, then they know they didn't just get an off-the-shelf item, but a customized creation, one personally made exclusively just for them. (Yes, I may have used that line once or twice during the hot August days.)

Unless you're a start-up entrepreneur, this "wearing of many hats" work environment is probably foreign to you (although you should try a limited version of it – it works wonders with the boss). There is a world outside the pizza stand. There are carnies, vendors, competitors, suppliers, Fair officials, Fair participants,... in short, a whole litany of constituency groups waiting for you to discover. I saw my grandfather work his magic with these groups. He kept tabs on their needs and wants and, should he be able to provide either of these, he would gladly do so.

There's a psychological term for this "scratch my back I'll scratch yours" phenomenon. Robert Cialdini, a renowned researcher and writer on behavior psychology describes it as "reciprocation." (You can read about it in any of his three best-selling books. Although all are great, I recommend *Influence: The Psychology of Persuasion.*) It's also the basis for the opening scene of *The Godfather.* Don Corleone agrees to help Bonasera, the undertaker, deal with some ruffians who took advantage of his daughter. He then tells Bonasera, "Some day, and that day may never come, I will call upon you to do a service for me." Usually, reciprocity is never this overt – it sort of ruins the good will of it – but it's the same idea.

The best way to get to the point where you can share the benefits of reciprocity is to make a lot of connections. More importantly, the only way to make a lot of connections is to find a lot of dots. What are the dots? More appropriately, "who" are the dots? They are friends, followers,... – whatever you call them. The key takeaway is the more people you know, the more likely you'll discover that one critical connection that stands between you and success.

The best way to collect a lot of "dots" is to involve yourself in a lot of activities. If you are fortunate enough to work in the front of the pizza stand, the dots come to you. I can't tell you how many customers visited the stand and bought pizza because they were in the same club, the same organization, or the same community as my grandparents.

Of course, if you've got an ethnic background like I do, there's no bigger connection than family. That whole mix up I described in Chapter 4 ("High Noon at the Erie County Fair") about the old woman looking for "Lena's son" exemplifies this. The pizza stand was like Grand Central Station as myriads of cousins and great aunts and great uncles – and all their friends – formed a never-ending parade in the front, side, and rear of the stand.

Needless to say, connections can do a lot of crazy things. If I had been thinking multi-generationally instead of multi-tasking with my eyes, I might have nipped this "Lena's son" confusion in the bud. But, then, there would have been no story to tell.

Lesson #11: Sometimes Multi-Tasking Will Find You... – Be prepared to go it alone for a while, especially if you plan on becoming an entrepreneur.

This means being prepared to do a couple of key jobs simultaneously. Even in larger organizations, a key player can get sick or go on vacation. The person who steps up to fill the gap (and still perform his original job well) is the person they'll look at first when it comes time for promotions.

Lesson #12: ...and Sometimes You'll Find Multi-Tasking – You're only one critical connection from becoming the success you've always dreamed of becoming. Connections can be people, events, ideas or any one of many (usually) unexpected things. The best way to collect more connections is to meet more people. This means becoming more active in your physical community. This means becoming more engaged in your on-line community. This means traveling to events outside your community. Ultimately, you want to live life to the fullest.

Lesson #13: Leave No Stone Unturned – You know what stones I'm talking about. It's your job to add them to your to-do list, find them and see what's under them. Have fun with others (that way they'll be more likely to remember you). Never turn down an opportunity to try something new. Who knows the people you'll meet, the places you'll go, and the idea's you'll imagine.

Unfortunately, many people confuse living life to the fullest with the meaning of life. They'll cut corners, fail to pay attention, and miss deadlines. All in all, they're forgetting an important personal value, the one that underlies all our success. I'll reveal it in the next chapter.

12. WORK HARD

My brother was in charge of making the pizzas. He'd assemble them. He'd bake them. Then he'd hand them off to me for cutting into eight evenly sized slices to sell to the hungry customers. We tried to be as efficient as possible – as easy as possible. But it's a fine line between efficiency and cutting corners. Early in our tenure, as my brother was trying to perfect his assembly style, my grandfather spied him doing something wrong. After a brief outburst, he proceeded with the day's lecture.

"Let me tell you something about taking short-cuts," he began. "I grew up in the very Italian west side of Buffalo. One day after school – I must have been a little younger than you are now – I was walking home and decided to take a short-cut. That short-cut required me to walk through an Irish neighborhood. I was all by myself and I didn't think it was a big deal. All of the sudden, a group of Irish kids came up and surrounded me. They asked me where I lived. I pointed towards the West Side. 'Are you a Dago?' asked one of the bigger kids. I told them I was Italian. They beat the hell out of me." His voice tailed off, as if prepared to sum things up. Instead, he asked, as if testing us, "Do you know the lesson I learned that day."

To be honest, Kenny and I didn't know what he was trying to say. Kenny took a stab. He said, more asking than declaring, "Don't ever walk alone in an Irish neighborhood?"

"What? No!" screamed my grandfather. "The lesson is never take short-cuts! Always do things the right way the first time. If you take a short-cut, you're entering unknown territory, and you never know what unexpected dangers you'll meet up with."

Seriously, we still had no clue what getting beat up in an Irish neighborhood had to do with making pizza, but we knew what Grandpa meant. He meant, when you know how to do something, don't be lazy. Just do it. And keep doing it because the more you do the same thing the quicker you'll become at doing it. Don't break routine "just because." When you break routine, you risk discovering unwanted side effects.

It's not like he didn't want us to try new things. He just wanted us to think about why we're trying a new thing. The worst reason to try a new thing was because we thought it was easier than what we were doing. Time and time again, in different ways, we'd test this notion of "easy" with my grandfather.

Nothing is as easy as it seems. That may sound like a downer, but there's a corollary that might just float your boat: Sooner or later, hard work will pay off. The trouble is, most people just can't shake off this "it's a sure thing" mentality. They're always looking for the easy way out. They're never suspecting the catch. This is why con games have been one of the most lucrative (for the con-artist) form of entertainment since Noah convinced two of every species to go on a six week cruise with him. According to his biographer Arthur H. Saxon, (Brooks, Andree, "Debunking the Myth of P. T. Barnum", *The New York Times*, October 3, 1982), P.T. Barnum never said, "There's a sucker born every minute." But there are.

And, as a wide-eyed teenager, I was certainly one of them, although maybe not for the usual reason. You see, I had this knack for relying on math, perhaps a little too much. I could calculate figures quickly in my head. This would often lead me to knowing the apparent value of a transaction faster than others. I could therefore make decisions more rapidly. This gave me an edge in games like chess. I found it also put me at an advantage when trading baseball cards.

This self-confidence, however, can lead to over-reaching – and that's precisely what con-men are taught to look for. The best mark is someone convinced they've got a sure-fire winning strategy. Of course, the Fair wouldn't allow out-right con games, but carnival games are still businesses. They need to entice you, but they need to make money. Here's what I mean.

To this day, I loved watching people play the "Guess Your Weight" game. There are several variations on this theme. The barker can guess your weight, or your age, or your birth month. With all those combinations, it's got to be a sure fire winner, right? And just look at those huge prizes surrounding the little booth with its carnival-like scale. Those gigantic furry bright multi-colored animals dangling from strings above the barker's head just beg you to play the game.

There's only one catch – you can't win the big prize until you've accumulated enough smaller prizes. The small prizes don't look bad by themselves, they just look bad in comparison to the humongous prizes orbiting the stand.

Still, it looked to my young mind as an impossible-to-lose proposition – and I had three premises to support my thesis. My grandfather made no pretense about his academic prowess. He just knew what was right and what was wrong. And he believed carnival games were wrong. I think he focused only on the monetary portion of the equation. He never quite appreciated the romantic value (q.v., picture the viral boyfriend, one arm carrying the larger-than-life cute furry animal while his adoring girlfriend snuggles ever closer to him wrapped around his other arm).

Needless to say, he had no problem shooting down my premises one-by-one. My first premise: "It's almost impossible to guess your weight, even within the allowable range." Grandpa's response: "The scale was rigged." I couldn't prove or disprove this one way or another, so I moved on.

My 2nd Premise: "Some people don't look their age, so they are sure fire winners." Grandpa's response: "It's actually easier to guess a customer's age not only through physical appearance, but by asking a few casual questions." OK, this one I could actually test. One day I furtively spied on a particular "Guess Your Weight..." booth. Grandpa was right. The fellow engaged in "innocent" banter with the customer and, more often than not, correctly guessed that person's age within the seemingly narrow spread. At the end of the day, I asked the carny how he could be so good at guessing. He confirmed what my grandfather said.

Why did he tell me his secret? I tell you where to find the answer at the end of this chapter. In the meantime, let's consider my final supposition.

My 3rd Premise: "While there are physical attributes that might indicate weight and age, your birth month is purely random." Grandpa's response was simply this: "Ask the carny how much the prizes cost and do the math." So I did. I went to the same carny who spilled the beans on the second premise, By now he recognized me. We exchanged pleasantries. In fact, I employed some of the conversational techniques he had revealed to me earlier. I was wondering if he was just as unsuspecting a mark as his clients.

Finally, I asked him, almost as an aside, "So, how much do these things cost you anyway." I pointed to the small prizes one must collect by the armload in order to obtain a single big prize.

It was late in the night and the Fair was closing down. The carny's eyes quickly scanned the immediate vicinity. No one was within listening distance. Under his breath, but into the microphone, he whispered, "About a penny." And then he quickly changed the subject.

There's a 1 in 12 chance the carny would correctly guess the birth month. Statistically, for every 12 customers, the carny would correctly guess one and miss on 11. Each customer paid the carny $1 to play. The carny therefore took in a total of $12 for 12 customers. The cost of one prize is, let's be charitable and say it's 5 cents. The carny awarded one prize at a cost of 5 cents. Therefore, for every 12 customers, the carny had net a marginal profit of $11.95 or an incredible 240% return. Grandpa was on to something.

Why did he tell me his secret? The answer lies at the end of the next chapter.

So work hard. Nothing is ever as easy as it appears. Only by diligently minding your business' processes will you succeed. Don't let either unscrupulous people or the blur of events overcome you. Finally, in order to get what you want, you've got to know what you want. Sometimes setting your goal is the hardest thing of all.

Lesson #14: The Odds are Never in Your Favor – You saw the most incredible deal in an ad on the TV. A local store is having a sale from 10:00 am until noon this Saturday. It's a steal! You've got to go buy one (or more). You tell all those connections (family, close friends) you've learned to make from the previous chapter about this sale. Sometimes those deals are real deals. Most times, however, you get what you pay for. There's no such thing as a free lunch, so stop wasting your time looking for one. Instead, work hard at doing the things you know will pan out in the end.

Lesson #15: Nothing Sells Itself – Just because you're there doesn't mean the people walking by will buy from you. We'll deal with the actual art of the deal and the sales process later on in this book. This is about more than the process, this is about the execution – that's what you need to work hard at. I got to see plenty of people every day from my perch at the front of the pizza stand. If I wasn't up to speed for some reason (it happens) and didn't want to risk making a mistake with a customer, I kept my mouth shut. Usually the people left me alone. If I was amped and wanted sell some slices of delicious (and nutritious) fresh hot-out-of-the-oven pizza, why then I'd work hard to attract attention from anybody. Yes, people who didn't intend on buying pizza stopped, listened, and bought some pizza. Lots and lots of times. In case it's not clear, this really works.

Lesson #16: Always Count the Cups – Trust, but verify. While nearly everyone I dealt with was nice, clean, and honest, I did see a few stray cats. Just because a vendor says there are six 50-cup packages in the box doesn't mean there are six 50-cup packages in the box. This really happened. The supplier came up and shorted us a stack of 50-cup packages. My grandmother caught the guy before he left and he made good on our order. As far as trust goes, when the guy left I just stared at my grandmother in disbelief that someone would so boldly try to rip us off. My grandmother casually gazed back and said, plainly, "Always count the cups." Then she went back to her seat in the doorway at the rear of the stand. This sound advice works everywhere. To this day, I don't leave the drive-thru window without double checking to make sure the entire order is there. By the way, there's an entire chapter on who not to trust – and it's not the next chapter.

Lesson #17: Pizza Doesn't Make Itself – Every once in a while my grandfather would walk into the stand and see me and my brother sitting and doing nothing. He'd admonish us, warning "the pizza doesn't make itself." We figured he just wanted to keep us on our toes. Depending on the time of day, my brother was usually pretty good at having 4-6 pizzas assembled and ready for baking. While his comment addressed the pizza, he really meant to include everything. He wanted us to constantly keep tabs on our current inventory. (We constantly did.) He wanted us to always plan ahead for the next rush. (We always did.) But, pretty much, he didn't want to see (and he didn't want potential customers to see) us sitting doing nothing. OK, I admit, it got hot in that stand and, since we didn't like to leave for fear of missing something, after working hard to make sure everything was in order we often needed to rest our feet every now and then. We usually worked hardest at the same time our grandfather was out working hard to promote the stand. As a result, he usually only saw us when we were sitting down, not when we were working hard.

Lesson #18: You Won't Get Something Unless You Ask for It – This might sound a lot like "Nothing Sells Itself" and there is a bit of an overlap. This lesson, though, covers everything, not just selling. It covers buying. It covers leisure activities. If covers entertainment choices. Most importantly, it covers your own personal goals. You won't attain those goals unless you know what they are. When we first started working at the stand, my grandfather would order enough boxes of pizza shells (the kind of pre-made frozen dough that everybody used then) to meet that days sales targets. Only, he didn't tell us until we asked him how he knew how many boxes to order. Once we knew that, we knew what the target sales goal for the day was. We made a game out of hitting that goal. Whether he intended it or not (and he probably did intend it), by revealing to us why he ordered that particular number of pizza boxes, he motivated me and my brother to meet his own goal. Without that motivation, on those really hot days, we might otherwise have sat in the shade in the back of the stand. (While I would have otherwise done that. Since he was in the back of the stand already, Kenny would sit there anyway.)

These personal values allow you to succeed in a manner that at the very least will satisfy your own desires. Life – and business – is about more than just pleasing yourself. If you want to implement the best practice when it comes to attracting people to your business, you've got to serve as a role model for the greater community. Our next section covers community values, starting with the one that defines the Erie County Fair itself.

PART III

COMMUNITY VALUES

– Justice –

13. THE CARNY CODE

There's nothing like a carnival atmosphere to learn the unadulterated truth about business and finance. And there's no better place for a carnival atmosphere than the Erie County Fair. It's a cauldron of commerce. Everywhere you turn, there's bartering, dickering, self-promoting, and, more than anything else, money and merchandise changing hands. It's the wild west of capitalism. Go there. You'll discover the most fundamental truth of the economic engine that powers our nation: A market that's free – untouched by the handcuffs of overburdening regulations – thrives. And a thriving economy leaves everyone happy – the sellers, the suppliers, the customers, and the sponsors.

We'll talk more about the economics of the carny in Chapter 20 ("The Art of the Sale"). For now, we want to focus on the philosophical foundation of the carny life, and what it taught me about life in general. The surprising truth about the carny life is that it applies to everyone, not just carnies. Like The Force, and just about everything else in the universe, there are two sides to this philosophy – a Dark Side and a good side.

Why You Should Never Trust a Carny

Carnies focus on only one job: To separate you from your money. Remember my grandfather's abhorrence of carnival games? My grandfather once sat me and my brother down and told us the story behind it. It occurred many years before we worked at the Fair, but after my grandfather had started the pizza stand. One evening, my grandfather's brother-in-law (that's my great uncle for those keeping score at home) came to visit my grandparents at the stand. My great uncle was sad. He had set his eyes on winning this TV being offered as a prize by one of the games. In the course of retelling his woes, he told my grandfather he had spent $50 trying to win that TV.

My grandfather exploded. He reamed out my great uncle (who was younger than him). "How could you spend $50 on something worth only $25?" ("I was so close to winning a lot of those times.") "Don't you know only fools play those games?" ("Then there must be a lot of happy fools.") "Do you see anyone walking around with a TV that he won?" ("I'm sure it's too heavy to walk with.") "Get out of here! Go home! And if you ever come back, don't bring any money!" ("OK, OK,... uh, could I still get a slice of pizza?") "Why should I give you a slice of pizza, you just spent all your money playing some game."

And my great uncle left, feeling a bit chastised – or so my grandfather said.

But the story didn't end there. Grandpa might have been really mad at my great uncle, but he downright vilified whoever was responsible at the game in question. So he left the stand in a huff – right in the middle of a busy rush! Everyone thought he went to go cool off somewhere. Fifteen minutes later he comes back, reaches into his pockets and pulls out $50 worth of quarters. He gives it to my grandmother, telling her to keep it and give it to my great uncle the next time she sees him.

Yes, so the story goes (and my grandfather never did reveal the sordid details), he found the proprietor of the offending game. After some "quiet" words in that clever, strong, and business-like manner of my grandfather, (no doubt combined, as needed, with his intimidating Svengali stare), he ended up getting all my great uncle's money back. This is the stuff of legend. This is what heroes are made of. Afterwards, it was clear to everyone in the family – and beyond – that my grandfather was not merely an honest citizen, but a Superman of sorts, helping those who needed help. Needless to say, after the episode with my great uncle, my grandfather became convinced all carny games were rigged. No one ever had the guts to disagree with him.

Except for me and Kenny. My brother and I were too young to have seen, first-hand, this event unfold. We had to learn for ourselves that, even when you're convinced you can win – and do win – the carny always wins in the long run. So, every once in a while, Kenny and I would challenge our grandfather's assumption. I've already told you the story about the Guess Your Weight/Age/Birth Month Game. But there are two other times when the subject of games came up.

I always liked the I-Got-It! game. Of all the games at the Fair, this one seemed the most evenhanded. More important, the prizes weren't those throw-away trinkets only kids like. No, these were prizes adults covet, although, as a kid, they didn't interest me. They were practical. They were something that most people wanted. In the real world, they were reasonably priced you could easily believe they were of half-way decent quality. All in all, these were the "TV" prizes of my era. Heck, even my grandmother salivated at the thought of obtaining that electric frying pan she always wanted.

Still, Grandpa put his foot down. "I do not want to see you playing that game or any other game," he'd say.

I wasn't going to take "no" for an answer. "But Grandpa," began my rebuttal, "It was like BINGO. If BINGO is good enough for the Catholic Church it has to be an impartial game."

My grandfather merely agreed, "Exactly. It's like BINGO."

Touché!

Truth be told, except for I-Got-It! I really never had any desire to play those traditional Fair games. I played them once when I was a kid, and that was good enough for me. The real games that attracted the attention of Kenny and me were the video games. We insisted, day in and day out, these games weren't rigged. What's to rig? After all, there were no prizes.

Remember, my grandfather ran a pizzeria. He could have had any number of arcade games if he wanted. If anyone was familiar with how to rig an arcade game, it was my grandfather. In fact, he only had one arcade game in his restaurant. It was one of those bowling games. With that game, there was no chance of a random "tilt" or an "unfortunate" bounce of a pinball. And, since customers played against each other, what would be the point of rigging the bowling game?

My grandfather wasn't familiar with the nature of the (then) new invention of video games. He assumed they were like all other arcade games. He thought they were just out to steal our money. Moreover, the fact they offered no prizes made us, in his eyes, even greater fools. So, one day, to prove his point, he gave me and Kenny four quarters (that's two each). He told us to go play our games, but come back as soon as we were done. He wanted to show us how fast these games ate our money.

We left.

And we didn't come back until an hour later.

Livid, Grandpa yelled at us. "I thought I told you to come back as soon as you were done playing the game."

"We did," we responded curtly (but respectfully) and proceeded to hand him three quarters.

His face morphed from angry to stunned. "You played one game for one hour for only twenty-five cents?"

"Yep," was all we said before going back to our usual stations in the stand.

Playing carnival games is like playing in a casino. (Ironically, the Hamburg Fairgrounds now houses a year-round Casino.) The odds are always stacked in the House's favor. This doesn't mean you should never play. The key word here is "play." Remember: It's all about entertainment, not winning. For some reason, Grandpa didn't tell us the story of the $50 TV until after he was sure we learned the lesson.

Why You Should Always Trust a Carny

Carnies have an honorable moral ethic. It's sort of why everyone associated with the Fair becomes part of the same family. In many ways, the Carny Code shares similarities with the Cowboy Code. It's about trust, loyalty, and protecting the herd. It's a professional philosophy that binds all guild members. In its own way, it inspires many of the lessons we introduced in Chapter 9 ("Family First").

Like all member-based creeds, one of the most important tenets is the differentiation between members and non-members. Here's how I discovered this "them" vs. "us" attitude. During my first few days working at the Fair, I would remove my pizza stand gear (apron and hat) and walk the Fair as any normal civilian would. Seen as a prospective customer, carnies along Midway row would regularly hound me. To be honest, I secretly enjoyed saying "no" to them. Of course, their approaches didn't matter because I usually didn't have any free money to spend anyway.

One day I forgot to take my hat off. An odd thing happened. As I walked my usual route, no carnies bothered me. They smiled. They waved. But they didn't move off their comfortable chairs the way they normally would. At first I didn't notice it. Then one carny finally barked at me. He cut himself short when he noticed my pizza stand hat. "Oh, you're one of us," he abruptly said and moved his eyes to real prospects.

From that point on, I always wore my pizza stand gear. Carnies no longer viewed me as a "them." carnies now considered me one of "us." That's how I got to know them. That's how I got to know some of their secrets, (only a few of which I've revealed in this book.) Incidentally, I never told my grandmother about my new friends. I'm sure she would have immediately told my mother. Once my mother found out who I was hanging with – Boom! – so long to my working in the pizza stand at the Erie County Fair.

Lesson #19: Every Person, Every Organization, and Every Idea has a Good Side and a Bad Side – Hollywood likes to play up the evil side of the carny. But, then again, Hollywood likes to play up the evil side of all businessmen. A carny is just another businessman. Like anything else, there's a Yin and Yang of good and bad rolled up in that mix. And, like anything else, when presented with such a mix, you try to play up to and bring out the good side. That's the side to be friends with, do business with, and to otherwise promote. That's not to say you shouldn't recognize and be mindful of the bad side. You might try to change it, but that's not always possible, nor is it necessarily a good idea. There's this thing called "free will." It's the basis of our moral code.

Lesson #20: It's Just as Important to Have Fun as it is to Make Money – Working long, hard, hours naturally induces stress. Play offers a certain entertainment value. Entertainment means having fun. Fun relieves stress. Less stress means you can work long, hard, hours. Lather, Rinse, Repeat. For me and Kenny, playing video games was all about the entertainment. We sought no material gain from the experience. We only wanted to sit back, relax, and enjoy the show. Once our grandfather realized that purpose, he never again bothered us about playing video games.

Lesson #21: A Greater Commonality Binds Us All – Find the ways you are most like the group you want to be a part of. Let that group know about it through your dress, your actions, and your voice. They'll look out for you, but there's a caveat: You need to look out for them.

The Carny Code is our constitution – our creed. It is the philosophy by which we all abide and live by. Oddly, this idea of a universal philosophy could only come about if we first learned and agreed upon a common tongue. We did. And it may be so obvious to you once you read the next chapter you'll wonder why you didn't think of it in the first place!

14. THE UNIVERSAL LANGUAGE

Kenny and I found it easier to engage in idle chatter with Grandma. Of course, unless she had just come from a confrontation with someone trying to rip her off, she had a propensity to sugar-coat the truth. When she actually wanted us to listen to her, the sugar got a little bit more practical. But it was still sugar.

In contrast, my grandfather had not met a public policy discussion that he felt worthy of discussing. When it came to practical, he wrote the book. I had a boxing coach like him. One time I asked my boxing coach how far away one should stand from one's opponent. He said, "Six feet." I said, "Six feet?! But's that's longer than my reach." My boxing coach simply replied, "Yeah, you never know if the other guy's carrying a knife."

His point was overbearingly practical. I was asking a question as if I might find myself in a boxing ring. My boxing coach knew it was far more likely I'd find myself in the shadows of a vacant alley. There, you never do know if the other guy has a knife.

My grandfather was just like that. He was eminently practical. Nothing explains this better than the story of the dollar fisherman. The Fair always had a carnival atmosphere – and its fair share of carnival characters. No group exemplified these characters more than the itinerant salesmen. Often dressed as clowns, they would roam the Fair selling the kind of worthless knickknacks kids would constantly bug their parents to purchase. One day, one of these fellows, in unsuspicious plain clothes, decided to offer his wares in the general vicinity of the pizza stand. It was a trick dollar bill – a real dollar bill attached to the end of a nearly invisible string. People would see this apparently loose dollar bill on the ground, stealthily look around to see if anyone was looking, then bend over to snatch the money. Only before they got their hands on it, the vendor would yank the string and the dollar would go flying away. You could depend on this prank to generate a good laugh and the vendor would use this as the opportunity to sell the toy to the victim.

It so happened that my grandfather came ambling back from one of his journeys just as the trick-dollar man was doing his thing. As my grandfather waddled towards the stand, waving hello to the sausage man in the stand next to ours, he caught sight of the dollar bill. He walked over to it, looked around to see if he could spot a likely owner, then began to bend over. Just as the vendor yanked the string, my grandfather slammed his foot on the bill. The string detached, leaving the surprised vendor with nothing but a piece of string. My grandfather proceeded to pick up the dollar, stuff it in his pocket, and return to the rear of the stand, completely oblivious to the situation, or at least so it appeared.

He displayed the same obliviousness to political causes and popular causes in general. When it came to the issues of the day, he'd never give the answer to those questions. He'd give you the answer to the question you should have asked. He was blunt, practical, and wasn't afraid to show his displeasure if he thought you should already know the answer.

As so it was, one unusually quiet afternoon, with the sun too hot to walk in, we – me, my brother and my grandfather – found ourselves in the shade of the pizza stand. Kenny and I were sitting talking and Grandpa was going through inventory. A neighboring vendor popped his head in the front of the stand. He was on break. When he was on break, he liked to come over to talk to my grandfather. Like my grandfather, this guy was the boss of his stand. Unlike my grandfather, this guy didn't own the stand.

Out of the blue, this guy starts going off on some racist rant. My grandfather kept his mouth shut and just nodded. The guy left. My brother and I were confused. Maybe we were naïve, but we couldn't understand why this guy said what he said. We were old enough to remember the race riots of the 1960s, but we were young enough to know there was no difference between people of different skin color. That was so obvious to us we couldn't fathom why people of either race would think otherwise. So we asked our grandfather to explain.

He was very familiar with ethnic stereotyping and the clashes of different cultures. He used ethnic stereotyping to his advantage, as it came in handy to be Italian if you're selling pizza. Regarding the clash of cultures, well, remember his experience taking a short-cut through that Irish neighborhood.

He began to explain to us, in his own terms, why the race riots happened and why some people had these racist feelings. As for his own beliefs, he was careful to stay neutral on the subject. As with the story of his unfortunate journey into Little Ireland, this one confused us, but we continued to listen.

"So, you wanna know what color is right?" he finally summed up.

We knew well enough not to answer. Black? White? Either way we'd be wrong. We knew there had to be a trick to this question, so we conceded and asked for the answer. This time I took the lead. "Yeah!" I answered, with a sort of tentative enthusiasm.

"Chris," he said with a most serious face, "there's only one color that matters in this world, and that's green."

My grandfather wasn't a greedy miser. No. What he was telling us – and this is what we understood even back then – is that it doesn't matter what ethnic group a person falls in. They all like to eat pizza. And they all pay for that pizza with money. And the color of that money is green. In the end, for whatever the differences in their outward appearances, they all speak the language of commerce, and the color of that language is green.

That didn't mean we never experienced a racist situation at the pizza stand. Late one evening, near closing time, my aunt took over for me in the front of the stand. She was starting to cleaning up so we could close the stand. I wasn't quite out of the stand yet, when a man – tall, muscular, and handsome – came staggering up to the stand. He was staggering because, well, let's say he must have had a really good time in the beer tent.

Towering over my tiny aunt, he asked her for a slice of pizza. My aunt told him we were out of pizza and that we were closing up. (We really were out of pizza and we really were in the process of closing up.)

This man refused to believe her. He claimed we had pizza but didn't want to serve him because of his ethnic origin. And then he augmented this verbal form of bullying with a more physical form. In a flash he started trying to climb over the plywood counter in the front of the stand. Fortunately, my uncles were also working in the stand that night. Fulfilling their family duty to protect their sister, they immediately converged on where this guy was trying to break through. I lunged forward to help, but Grandma put her arm on my shoulder to stop me.

This time, though, it's not like when she squeezed my brother's hand to hold him back from the drunk steel worker. This time, she stops me only to grab my aunt and shove her behind me. She tells me to stay away from the front, my uncles will take care of the intruder. My job was to make sure I stay between the invader and my aunt. Again, the instructions and intent are quite different from what she told Kenny in that earlier story of the late-night encounter in the parking lot. This wasn't about protecting money. This was about protecting life and limb.

Ultimately, my uncles forced the trespasser down from the pizza stand and we quickly brought the plywood shutters down and secured them. We, however, stayed in the stand because the drunk man continued to loiter. Finally, a policeman came by (remember my grandfather's uncanny ability to provide them a free pizza just when they were the hungriest?) and told us he'd watch the pizza stand. Seeing a uniformed officer of the law did the trick. The errant inebriant wandered off towards the Midway.

Had we have had any pizza left, we would have gladly served him, no matter his ethnic heritage, no matter the condition of his liver. The only color that mattered was green. But when he went into full bully mode, that changed everything. My uncles did what they had to do to stop a bully – secure the perimeter. It was only after we took care of protecting ourselves that my grandfather went to the police. Only *we* could best stop the bully during the actual attack. The police are best used to prevent a known bully from attacking again.

Lesson #22: Race, Religion, and Politics have No Place in Business – If you want your business to be successful, ignore social issues. Even the most honorable of social issues still upsets half of the population. Why put your business in the position of losing 50% of your potential customers? It's better to remain agnostic to the customers' personal beliefs. This is the ultimate "Don't Ask, Don't Tell" policy.

Unfortunately, recent developments by social agitators make it difficult for targeted businesses to remain agnostic on social issues. They're placed in a position where, if they remain silent, they're making a statement. I think my grandfather would say, "My politics are my personal business, not yours. How I operate my business is my personal business, not yours. Now, do you want to buy a slice of pizza or not, because you've got a long line of hungry people behind you who are waiting to be served." Then he would call his police friends over to make sure the person doesn't continue to harass the workers (his family), the customers (his extended family), or loiter near the stand (ultimately, his most enduring gift to both his family and extended family).

Lesson #23: If Someone Breeches Your Front Lines, You're in a Lot of Trouble – The moment the man tried to scale our front wall, the entire male contingent in the stand went into action. Even my grandmother got into the act, but as a general, not as a soldier on the front line. This story is a metaphor for what many businesses face, either from direct competition, bad news, or even the agitators I spoke of in Lesson #22. Many people and many businesses have a line of defense which protects them. Once that line is penetrated, unpleasant things can happen. You need to know what resources you have to defend that line, how they will be deployed, and who will deploy them. Because of a small hole in its left wing, upon re-entry the Space Shuttle Columbia succumbed to the penetration of hot gases – through *that* hole, a hole no more than a few inches big. Find your holes. Plug them. *Then* get the authorities involved.

Lesson #24: In Case of a Fire, Know the One Thing You're Taking with You – Your business has lots of assets. Some of them can withstand a fire. Some of them can be replaced if lost in a fire. A few of them can neither withstand the fire nor be replaced. Those are the ones you need to protect the most. In our two stories involving drunks, one involved something that can be replaced – money. It's not worth risking life and limb over money. You can always get more. The other story involved something that cannot be replaced – my aunt. There are going to be some times when you have to protect something at all costs – including life and limb. My grandmother clearly thought it was worth risking my life and limb to protect my aunt. And I was honored that she put me in the position to do it.

It used to be only lawyers could speak a different language even though they spoke the same language. More and more, it seem like everyone else is giving this a try. That might work for one-on-one conversations, but, when you're in the "Biz," you better talk, do, eat, and breathe the way the audience understands it should be done. Ironically, while this may sound stultifying, at the Erie County Fair it's liberating. You'll see why in the next chapter.

15. LIFE IS A BIG SHOW

K, OK, so Shakespeare may have said this better:

> *"All the world's a stage,*
> *And all the men and women merely players.*
> *They have their exits and their entrances,*
> *And one man in his time plays many parts."*
>
> – Jaques, *As You Like It*, Act II scene vii

Hmm, that has the ring of multi-tasking, doesn't it? Maybe this Shakespeare fellow was on to more than he knew.

It's impossible to understate the importance of the performance, but what exactly does "performance" mean? It means you can never break character. Why? Because everyone is watching you all the time. If this sounds like today's world with the internet and social media and 24/7, then you are beginning to understand the concept of "performance."

Performance is especially important at the Fair. People going to the Fair expect to be entertained. As a participant in the Fair, you realize everyone around you is trying to entertain. That means you have to compete for the Fairgoer's attention. Ultimately, if you want to work in "The Show," you better be prepared to let loose of those inhibitions that have been holding you back.

There are a number of rules to follow if you want to ensure you are providing an engaging performance:

1. Be different
2. Be loud
3. Be consistent

4. Be different
5. Be creative
6. Oh, and did I say "be different."

When it comes to performing, you only have one objective: Stand out and get attention. Everybody working at the Fair wants to get the Fairgoer to notice him. For the most part, Fairgoers expect to be wooed. Chances are, if they don't like being pursued, they're not going to the Fair in the first place. So the people that decide to attend the Fair already have a desire to be enticed. They are seeking to be courted. Think about it. This is the opposite of those "no-call" lists.

What did this all mean for the pizza stand? My grandfather, first and foremost, was a businessman. Before owning a pizzeria, he owned a grocery store. All the while he worked regular shifts at the Steel Plant (at least when they didn't have massive layoffs). For fun, he was a member of the Lake Erie Club. He played cards, bocce, and the horses. As far as I know, he never had a desire to sing, dance, or act in any way, shape, or form. (Granted, being of Italian origin, he, like all of us, naturally spoke with animated gestures.)

That being said, he was just as much a good performance-oriented carny as the best of them. My grandfather became the personality that defined the pizza stand. And I'm not talking just about our pizza stand, but all pizza stands. Of all the pizza stand operators of Italian descent, he best looked the part, he best sounded the part, and he had the most outgoing personality. It also helped that he looked like the actor who played Frank De Fazio, Laverne's father on the then top-rated *Laverne & Shirley* show. (It further helped that Frank De Fazio operated a pizza parlor on the show. It was no help whatsoever but more of an amazing coincidence that my mother – remember her, the Lena I referred to earlier – possessed and wore the same cursive capital "L" brooch Laverne wore in the series). With all this Hollywood background, it was only natural that my grandfather would become a semi-famous personality for at least ten days a year.

His gimmick consisted of two props: A microphone and a pair of oversized novelty sunglasses. The microphone, and the speaker it was hooked up to, made practical sense. With the main entrance to the grandstand across from us, we had to compete with the loudest loud speaker the Fair had to offer. But – and this is a very important distinction – it was, more importantly, a prop. Think about this: How many times have you seen someone turn into a totally different person when you stick a microphone in their face? Well, he often used that microphone to "interview" passers-by. That was always good for more than a few chuckles as well as more than a few sales. That's the power of a microphone. That's the power of a prop.

Now, about those oversized novelty sunglasses. A prop is only as good as its ability to be seen. The microphone, was normally held low, making it hard to see in a crowd. It was also almost completely hidden by the hand holding it. This meant, depending on the color of your shirt (i.e., if it came close to matching the color of the microphone's head), the prop was almost impossible to see. Not so with the novelty sunglasses. First, they sat on your head, and heads were easy to see in a crowd. Second, they were huge, which meant they made your head look strange in a crowd. Third, they were a shade of bright green that you rarely saw in nature, which meant they stuck out like a sore thumb in a crowd. I didn't know what was more famous – my grandfather or those oversized novelty sunglasses. And he guarded them as if they were worth a fortune. In a way, they were.

Incidentally, if you've got a copy of the Monday, August 18, 1980 *Buffalo Courier-Express*, turn to page 3 of the local news section. There, in the upper right hand corner you'll see a picture Bob Willett took of my grandfather. Yes, he's wearing those oversized novelty sunglasses. And, yes, they spelled his name wrong. Not that the misspelling bothered him. After all, he misspelled his own name on the sign of his own business. He knew a picture was worth a thousand misspelled names.

My greatest honor was the day my grandfather first let me wear those glasses during my own barking sessions. I didn't need the speaker. I was young and active on the radio. As both an AM disc jockey (when AM still played music) and a play-by-play announcer (for my school's Division I football and hockey teams), my trained voice was loud enough to compete with the Fair's speakers. (In fact, one of my routines was to a have a "conversation" with the PA announcer, since the Fair announcements were often repeated and easy to memorize. This definitely got stares from the crowd.) Despite not needing the speaker, I still used the mike. After all, I needed something to use when I "interviewed" some innocent bystander. The fact the mike wasn't connected to anything, yet I faithfully acted as if it was, only improved the gag.

Lesson #25: Presentations Shouldn't Just be Informative, They Should be Entertaining – Picture the bland Dan Aykroyd plugging the *Blue Brothers'* big show while driving through neighborhood streets in Chicago. That's how most food vendors sold their products. They used canned recordings of monotone voices. We used live entertainment – either me or my grandfather. Not only did it get people's attention, but it showed them how different we were from everybody else. You could see their minds thinking, "If the workers are that vibrant, imagine how much tastier the pizza is!"

Lesson #26: Presentation Should Include Props, Not Just Personality – A catchy personality, even combined with funny jokes, will only get you so far. Props, though, can differentiate you from all other speakers. (File this under the category "And Now for Something Completely Different.") The effective use of props will get attention. If you pick the right prop, it can also send a message. For example, one of the slogans I barked while wearing the oversized novelty sunglasses was, "This pizza looks so good it makes my eyes pop out of my head!"

Lesson #27: No False Idols – This is an accessory to the idea that life is a big show. If we are all actors on the stage of life, then no one is a celebrity. If you act that way, you're more likely to be accepted as a peer by so-called "celebrities." It's easy to do. A celebrity is just like you and me, except more people know them. They just want to be treated like regular guys.

I don't know how many local celebrities my grandfather knew, but I know he knew quite a few, especially if they were Italian. He didn't treat them any different than anyone else. I think that made them feel more comfortable with him. Usually when they came to the stand, he would take them in back where it was a little bit more private. As a result, since I was in the front, I rarely heard the conversation.

As I mentioned earlier, WBEN occupied the space two places down from our stand. My grandfather knew most of the jocks who broadcast live from the Fair. He even got them to call my grandmother, live, on-the-air, when she was in the hospital. One day a somewhat popular local radio announcer took a break from his show and came to our stand. It was Jay Fredericks (who now goes by his real name Fritz Coleman and works as a weatherman in Los Angeles where he also doubles as a stand-up comedian – a career he started in Buffalo). He was closer to my generation (or my parent's) than my grandfather's, so my grandfather didn't know him.

I certainly recognized him. But, imitating my grandfather, I made no big deal. I was quite familiar with his voice, but I expected to hear a more normal voice. After all, I had a "radio voice" for on the air and a normal voice for speaking in the everyday world. When, however, he said "Two Pepsis, please," it came out in that smooth velvety baritone that I had long known. (Who knew? Sometimes that "Radio Voice" is also their real voice.) I made the usual small talk one expects from a Fair vendor and then he went back to his broadcast. I had so wanted to talk to him about our shared life as disc jockeys/radio producers, but I remembered my grandfather's model and kept my mouth shut. Did I miss an opportunity? Maybe. But I did keep the integrity of the stand and of the Carny Code intact.

There are celebrities, and then there are pretenders. Our Founding Fathers said all men are created equal. Problems arise when some men think they are more equal than others. The situation gets worse when that attitude derives from a position of power. Then it can, it may, and, oftentimes, it will be used against you. The next chapter explores an all too common malady that pollutes all of society. I was initially introduced to it first hand as told in the following story...

16. NEVER TRUST ANYONE CLAIMING TO BE FROM THE GOVERNMENT

Ronald Reagan was elected President of the United States right at the midpoint of my tenure working in the pizza stand at the Erie County Fair. Aside from the usual Kennedy shrine every good Catholic had, my grandparents didn't exhibit any outward political preference. Perhaps this was the result of my grandfather (both of them, as a matter of fact, since this is the event that caused them to first meet) being arrested as a "communist" while marching with the Steelworkers Union in a parade. (This is ironic given his career as a capitalist entrepreneur.)

I can't say if my grandparents were Reagan Democrats, but I do know they got a kick out of one of his jokes about the government. Reagan once said the ten scariest words were "Hello. I'm from the government and I'm here to help."

Long before Reagan's first campaign for President in 1976, my grandparents displayed these very sentiments. One morning a small man came to the stand. He had the build of a meek accountant. He had the dress of a meek accountant. He had the tiny voice of a meek accountant. He said a few words to my grandmother. Then he left. I had no idea who he was.

My brother and I asked my grandmother who the man was and what did he want. She just said it didn't matter, but if he comes back, don't say anything.

A few hours later, the man showed up again, this time with a taller fellow. The taller guy looked just like the shorter guy. The taller guy didn't say a word. The shorter guy was definitely trying to convince my grandmother of something. My grandmother feigned ignorance. She also casually asked for some documentation to support the small man's claim. The man opened his satchel and produced a small piece of paper. My grandmother's countenance instantly changed, as if she just completed an inside straight. She's happy, but only Kenny and I can tell. To an outsider, her face barely changes.

"Oh, that's not us," she says. "Look, here, at the address. It's a totally different business. You can see they spell 'Salvatore' with an 'e.' We spell it without the 'e.' Salvatore is a very popular name, so we dropped the 'e' so people wouldn't confuse us with any of the others."

The man looked dumbfounded. But my grandmother was right and he knew he couldn't do anything about it. He could say nothing to refute my grandmother's plaintive logic. Convinced he had hit a dry hole, he handed my grandmother another piece of paper. "These are your taxes due for the Fair. You can pay me in cash."

"Oh, that's far more cash than we have," my grandmother lied. "Can I write you a check instead?"

The man frowned but said a check would be fine. My grandmother wrote him a check and handed it to him. The man's body took a start. "You're supposed to make the check to my name," he said.

"Oh," my grandmother said with all the naïve innocence she can conjure up, "I'm used to making my tax checks payable to the 'Sales Tax.'"

The man began to try to explain, but gave up before he started. He took the check and left. He had arrived at the pizza stand like a man with prize game in his sites. He walked away like a shamed dog, the taller man following behind him. The taller man never said a word the entire time.

Lesson #28: Never Give Them More Than What They Ask For – This is one of the biggest mistakes people make. They give the government more than what the government asks for. They do this "just in case they made a mistake." My grandmother, knowing in her gut she was right, could have easily paid the incorrect "Salvatore" (with an "e") bill knowing, sooner or later, someone would discover that "Salvator" paid the tax bill of "Salvatore." Once this happened, the figuring goes, the money would be refunded. When I asked her why she didn't do that, just to get rid of the guy, she laughed. "If you give them something more than they should get, don't count on getting that money back anytime soon!" "Besides," she added, "why put off until tomorrow a problem you can solve today?"

Lesson #29: Never Give Them What They Ask For – The tax man asked for cash. It wasn't that large and I knew we had enough to pay for it. Granted, it would have used up most of our spare change, and if we got several consecutive customers with twenty dollar bills at the beginning of the lunch rush, it would have wiped out the rest of it. Still, I asked her why she didn't give him cash. "He could have kept the cash himself, then come back to us saying we never paid. Worse, someone else could back to us saying we didn't pay. A check is proof you paid. Don't do something just because someone else tells you to. Do it because it's the right thing for you."

Lesson #30: Always Act Dumber Than You Are – It's better to always make the other guy feel he's smarter than you. That's when he'll make mistakes. That's when he'll cut you a break. Either way, your ego isn't worth that much. Focus on improving your self-worth, not your self-esteem. The taxman could have insisted my grandmother tear up the check made to the County and write a new one made out in his name. But, despite his own best efforts, she had already pointed to one mistake he made, so he didn't want to risk having her – even accidentally – find another, this time more fatal, mistake. When I asked her why she didn't make out the check in this man's name, she said, "Never make your tax payment out in the name of the agent, always make it out to the name of the agency." Again, she was afraid it was too easy for the man to cash it in his own account, leaving our tax balance listed as unpaid.

This last lesson may seem as if it applies only when dealing with government officials. In reality, it's really a subset of a much more important rule. It's a rule that ought to govern all your life's doings. I know there are famous examples that run counter to this rule, but it is an essential rule in business. It's a rule that's vitally important for start-up companies, as it can provide safety during the critical incubation period all successful entrepreneurs must survive. If it sounds like we're leaving the community section and heading into the business section, then you've got good ears. The next chapter – the first in the business section – explores the all-important trait we're describing here.

PART IV

BUSINESS VALUES

– The American Way –

17. HUMILITY

If all of us from the Greater Western New York region learned anything during the Buffalo Bills' Superbowl years, it was that, once we made it there, the rest of the league was gunning for us. Now, this usually happens to the teams that play in the Superbowl. The following season, everyone is gunning for them. Whether they won or lost the Superbowl, it doesn't matter. Those two teams have a big red target on their jerseys. From the mightiest of competitors to the weakest opponents, they'll all try to beat you if you were in the Superbowl last year.

Don't underestimate the power of this. Even a one-win team will consider their season a success if that one win came at the expense of the previous year's Superbowl contender. I remember, during all those back-to-back bad seasons the Bills had, there were a couple of things we'd point to with pride.

First, our only win in 1968 was against Joe Namath's soon-to-be Superbowl winning New York Jets. I still remember that game. It was a home game so we could only listen to it on the radio. That meant we could work outside and still catch the game. Kenny and I were really young then, but my father brought us along to "help" him lay the bricks for a new raised flower bed at my great-uncle's house.

Second, and more controversial, we were the only team with an honest-to-goodness chance to beat the Miami Dolphins in their undefeated year. Let me rephrase that. We were the only team that *beat* the Miami Dolphins in their undefeated season. If not for an errant fumble and an obviously erroneous call by the referee, the Bills beat the Dolphins. That's right. The ref awarded the game to the Dolphins. That's our story and we're sticking to it.

During the Bills run of four consecutive Superbowls (what's that, you say you're not aware they're the only team to have ever done it?), the red target on their jerseys seemed larger than normal. It was as if, not just all their opponents, but the entire nation – with the sole exception of Chris Berman – wanted to see the Bills defeated. This rallied the resilient team and, well, we've seen the consequences. In fact, Bruce Smith's memorable *Poltergeist* inspired "We're Baaack" continues to haunt NFL highlight films.

So, the Buffalo Bills and their fans have been on both sides of this equation. We've been both the ones with the target on their chest and the ones trying to knock off the team with the target on their chest. On the whole – and I think it's fair to say I speak for the entire region – we'd prefer to be the ones with the target on their chest.

But, as a business owner, it's best to leave the target to the other guys. At the pizza stand, we loved our pizza. We knew it was the best around and we weren't afraid to tell people. Heck, we were so brash we'd dare people to take a taste test! (Ironically, far from cocky, this was an example of cooperation with our competitors because, if we successfully convinced customers to take a taste test, both pizza sellers would benefit from increased sales.)

There was one thing we never bragged about. That was the business itself. In a way, no one expected us to brag about our business. After all, it was run by two elderly Italian immigrants. The profile said those in that category were dumb, poorly fed, and, in general, lacked a sense for business. You'd think this would have insulted my grandparents. Quite the opposite, they milked it for all it was worth. Remember the story of the drunk steelworker asking my grandfather about how much money we made that day? Recollect the story of the taxman who tried to trick my grandmother into giving him cash for someone else's tax bill? My grandparents had no problem playing dumb, acting feeble, and doing anything that would make the other guy appear smarter, stronger, and wiser.

Why? Because when they did that they knew they had him exactly where they wanted him. Bear in mind, though, they never played these mind games with sincere folks. They used these tricks only against people who thought they could get the better of "people" like my grandparents. In a very real sense, it was my grandparents' way of fighting for the little guy. They didn't have the conventional weapons of money and position. They just had a lot of street smarts. And they weren't afraid to use what they had. But they never admitted they had it – even after they used it successfully. Why paint a target on yourself if you don't need to?

Lesson #31: Bragging About How Good You Are Only Paints a Big Target on You – Trying to run a successful business is hard enough without unnecessarily creating even more obstacles. All you do by bragging is motivate your opponent. It's better to come across as a lessor adversary. Let the other guy think he's better than you. Who knows, maybe your opponent will let his guard down and reveal a key piece of information that can put you in a position to eventually win the day.

Lesson #32: A Stronger Foe will often Bypass a Weaker Opponent – In the days of chivalry, there was no honor in beating an obviously weaker opponent. It was even a sign of high moral character – in other words, charity – to subordinate yourself to a lesser. Believe it or not, for the most part, most moral folks still abide by these rules.

And sometimes not.

I'll have to go back to ancient times to explain. It's the story of Athens vs. Milos, a small conflict that was part of the much larger Peloponnesian War (which is often called "the war between Athens and Sparta" because some people don't think we can spell or pronounce the word "Peloponnesian"). For reasons that don't really matter to the story, it came to be that one day the Athenians gave the Melians (that's what the people from Milos called themselves) an ultimatum: Surrender and pay us tribute, or die. The Melians, being the smart Greeks they were, countered with a philosophical argument. "We are weak and you are strong," they began. "You prove nothing by defeating us, so why bother."

The Athenians, being even smarter when it comes to arguing philosophy (in case you didn't know, Socrates was involved in the war – on the Athenian side), said the opposite is true. "Because Milos was weaker than Athens," said the wise and powerful leaders of the Delian League, "Athens must destroy Milos if the Melians fail to surrender. Otherwise, others would see Athens itself as weak."

So Athens trashed Milos, permitting Thucydides, the father of "scientific history" and author of *The History of the Peloponnesian War*, to write the famous adage, "Right, as the world goes, is only in question between equals in power, while the strong do what they can and the weak suffer what they must."

Playing possum can get you out of that little problem with that big ol' grizzly bear, but it might also attract a vulture or two.

Lesson #33: Sympathy Leads to Sales –In case you're not familiar with the history of the region, "the Steel Plant" always referred to the Bethlehem Steel Plant. This was the largest employer in the area – upwards to 30,000 people – and covered a vast territory from Woodlawn through Lackawanna. There were about a half dozen major steel companies in the Buffalo area at one time. You always spoke of them by their proper name. When you referred to "the Steel Plant," however, everyone knew you meant the Bethlehem Steel Plant.

Despite his age – and I could never understand this – my grandfather didn't have seniority at the Steel Plant. As a result, during every layoff, his number would come up. This concerned a lot of my grandparents' friends. They felt bad for my grandparents. They wanted to help my grandparents. Therefore, they bought a lot of pizza from my grandparents.

Sometimes, the nicest thing you could do for people is to allow them to help you, even if you think you don't need the help. My grandparents never thought they needed help. My grandparents were nice to a lot of people. Humility implies a certain modesty, but it doesn't mean you can't be cool. The next chapter explains why.

18. GET COOL, BOY

I remember evenings when my grandfather would come home from work proudly telling my grandmother how much steel he lifted that shift. Steelworkers were rightfully proud of their work and, in my young eyes, it seemed like they each wanted to outdo the other at work. (No doubt Bethlehem Steel secretly – or not so secretly – encouraged this friendly internal competition.) One evidence of hard work: Dirty, sweaty clothes.

At the pizza stand, this sort of evidence was frowned upon. The rule of the day was "Never let them see you sweat." Well, Kenny could sweat. He was in the back. In the dark shade. He could get away with sweating. I was in the front. I couldn't sweat, no matter how hot the sun was.

We both had to keep our clothes clean.

But this part of "never let them see you sweat" is just being hygienic and leaving the customers with a clean professional image. There's another, more important, side of this coin.

Business is a tough world filled with tough guys playing a lot of tough games. These guys try to get you to sweat. They hope you break down. They want you to cede your turf to them. It's that dog-eat-dog attitude my grandfather was trying to convey in that Christmas Eve card game you read about in the Prologue. He taught his kids to be tough and survive. He wanted the same for his grandkids.

In the playground, you had to be physically tough. In the business world, you have to be mentally tough. And that meant staying cool. The minute you lost it – the minute you got mad – you lost. I can say my grandfather yelled at us and my grandmother hollered at us, but we never saw them lose their temper with anyone outside the family. That didn't mean they didn't get mad, and I already alluded to my grandfather's "angry eyes" regarding the poor game proprietor who convinced my great uncle to part with $50 in the vain hope of winning a television. They might have gotten angry, but they never lost it.

Not that they didn't have reason to. When my brother and I started working at the pizza stand, the stand had been relocated to the front of the Bazaar Building on the side of the track opposite the grand stand. For much, if not all, of the 1960's the family's stand had always been right outside of the grandstand's main entrance – prime real estate at the Fair. What happened to get banished to "no-man's-land" was a story never told to us. Rumor had it that a very competitive pizza vendor had cozied up to the Fair Committee. My grandfather's stand was the closest to her space – she was right at the top of the Avenue of Flags, about five spots to the west of us – so she convinced whatever powers that once were to move my grandfather.

When I first heard this, I got mad. Really mad. Sonny Corleone mad. My brother, too. What made us even madder was the fact my grandparents took it in stride. They never let the invisible other guys see them sweat about it. I could never understand that, until,... the next year. They were back at their old spot, and remained there until they moved to their current location at the top of the Avenue of Flags – an even better location. They never told us how they got their old spot back. All they said was that the Fair Committee had always been very kind to them.

Lesson #34: Violence Never Solved Anything – You might think the hot-headed Sonny Corleone was one cool cat, but all that bluster got him nothing save for a few dozen bullet holes and a nice funeral. If you're reacting, you're doing, not thinking, and that could lead you to make foolish decisions. Still not convinced? Then re-read the previous chapter.

Lesson #35: Patience is a Virtue – It's often better to sleep on it than to respond rashly. My grandparents didn't complain when the stand was moved. They slept on it. They slept on it for an entire year. In the end, the problem turned out not to be a problem. It just faded away to nothing. I used this lesson often during my stint as an elected official. I was more of a citizen-legislator (i.e., the ideal our Founding Fathers envisioned when they created this country – a merchant who merely took his turn serving, not someone who tried to make a career out of holding public office). Whenever I tried to do something that made common sense, the people (i.e., the voters, not the other elected officials) usually nodded their head in agreement. This made my opponents angry. They did things to try to get my goat. Instead of responding immediately in the heat of anger, I'd go home and sleep on it. By the next morning, the ire had subsided and I could more soberly determine what, if any, response was appropriate.

Incidentally, I once actually used the phrase "patience is a virtue" while working in another pizza stand. (This one wasn't at the Erie County Fair, it was at the old Silver Stadium, home of the Rochester Red Wings baseball team.) I had just graduated from high school and was trying to bring the spirit of my grandfather's pizza stand to this one. The customers were complaining because the pizza was taking too long to make. That's when I used the phrase – but in a humorous way. The owner of the concessions franchise wasn't pleased. He lost his cool. He broke up the stand the next day. In retrospect, the owner was so focused on making money ("winning") that he forgot he had to keep everyone else on his side, too. There's a famous phrase for that. It's a smart strategy for all successful businessmen (and negotiators and diplomats). We'll talk about it next.

19. JUST WIN, WIN BABY

In a large and growing market, competition is a fool's game. There are enough customers to satisfy a large number of diverse businesses. The cost of competing eats into the bottom-line. Competition therefore becomes a value proposition: Does the creation, maintenance, and promotion of a Unique Selling Proposition ("USP") add enough value to offset its costs? In the real world, it's rare to find a large, growing market. Competition is intense. You can't win if you don't have a USP. But we'll leave all that for the next chapter. This chapter is about those rare markets. It's also about the very thing you need no matter what kind of market you serve.

The Fair is different from most business environments. It has a limited time horizon. It has an easily measurable – growing but finite – market size. My grandparents told Kenny and me the Fair Committee itself oversees vendors to prevent oversaturation of any particular product category. We believed this was (and perhaps continues to be) done on purpose to allow vendors to worry less about making a profit – i.e., competition – and focus more on giving the customers the best possible Fair-going experience. The Fair, like any other limited event, is therefore more of a closed market than what we see in the real world. It's still a free market, but more in a limited sense.

Likewise, cooperation therefore becomes a value proposition: Will the long-term value of "playing nice" with the competitors offset any short-term loss in sales? During my era, my grandparents and, especially, my grandfather, tried to "play nice" with everyone – including the competition. For the most part, there was reciprocation. In the one case of the vendor who didn't cooperate, well, she traded short-term gains for long-term extinction. Her business exited the scene decades ago. It is no longer among the many long-time vendors that have made the Erie County Fair the success and the tradition that it remains today. Could her lack of cooperation have been the reason?

The real world limits cooperation between normally competing entities. The free market generally frowns on such collaboration because it can hurt consumers. Such collaboration can sometimes help consumers (think Beta vs. VCR and HD vs. Blu-Ray and pretty much any product requiring compatible technical standards). Regulators, however, assume such collaboration always hurts customers; thus, they aggressively seek to stymie it before it grows too large.

That being said, cooperation – so-called "win-win" scenarios – still rules the day. Little niceties go a long way to creating these scenarios. My grandparents learned early on in their Fair experience the power of networking. The pizza stand didn't begin as a stand at all. It began as a collection of local food vendors under a tent – sort of like a food court. During this period, they were new to being a Fair vendor and had to learn a lot and had to learn it quickly. The best way to learn quickly was to get veteran Fair vendors to share their secrets. The best way to get Fair veterans to share their secrets was to become friends with them. The best way to become friends with anyone is to be friendly yourself. My grandparents were very friendly.

My grandfather was great at making friends. Sometimes, my grandmother didn't trust all his "friends" – she thought they were only out to take advantage of him. I think my grandfather knew it was always possible some of his new "friends" were only friendly to get something from him, but he was inclined to give everyone the benefit of the doubt. Still, when it came down to it, he always trusted my grandmother's instincts ahead of his own.

Both my grandparents loved to give. My grandfather would often surprise people with a free pizza pie. He considered this both a courtesy and a show of respect – as well as free advertising since he thought (and we all knew) he made the best pizza at the Fair. He did not discriminate in his charity. He gave free pizza to everyone from the highest Fair official to the security guards working late at night when everyone else had gone home.

After all the complaints from my grandmother about his "friends" just wanting free pizza, one night, after a particularly long and exhausting day, we started our long trek down the Avenue of Flags when, all of the sudden, a golf cart driven by one of the night security guards came up and asked my grandparents if they wanted a ride. My brother and I ran beside them as they drove to the car parked in the seemingly distant Quimby lot. My grandmother never complained about my grandfather's friends again.

One act of giving perplexed my brother and me. Every time my grandfather went to the men's room, he'd give the attendant some money. All the pay toilets had been removed, so his giving the attendant money confused us. "Grandpa," we asked, "why do you always give that man money?"

"Because he has to eat," my grandfather would answer in a way that told us the answer was obvious.

This only confused us more. "But doesn't the Fair already pay this man? Doesn't he already earn enough money to pay for his food?" We just didn't get it.

My grandfather paused. He understood the reason for our confusion. "I don't give him money so he can buy food," he explained, "I give him money because, just like everybody else, he has to eat. And when he has to eat, I want him to eat pizza."

Then we understood.

But, for the most part, my grandfather used pizza as his currency. Late at night, my grandfather would regularly reduce the price – but not give away – on the night's last pizza for some random carny who would be spending the night in some James E. Strates tent city (or the equivalent therein).

Similarly, for all her bluster about giving away pizza for free, my grandmother had a heart of gold when it came to being nice to people in need. Every once in a while, a clearly downtrodden customer would come to the stand and meekly ask, "Can I buy a slice of pizza?" My grandmother, sensing the destitute situation of this person, routinely offered the slice at a discounted price or even gave it away for free. My brother and I could never figure out how she knew when to do this. Sometimes, from the rear of the stand, she would see me serve someone who she thought needed a break. I'd hand the person the slice and then ask the person for the payment "Seventy-five cents, please." Before money changed hands, I'd hear a small voice behind me say, "Chris, that slice only costs fifty cents." In reality, all our slices cost the same, but not when my grandmother was around. She knew those extra pennies meant more to the customer than they did to her. She felt God had blessed her with more than enough pennies and had no problem sharing a few with others.

Inevitably, the beneficiaries of my grandmother's good will would return, sometime years later and in a much better position. They'd retell their own personal story of my grandmother's (or grandfather's) kindness, introduce us to their family, then proceed to buy an entire pie. They'd also inform us that they had told all their friends to be sure to buy pizza at my grandparents' pizza stand.

The Fair was rife with these "you rub my back I'll rub yours" transactions. It was – and continues to be – a pleasure to see such a community work all together for the benefit of each participant.

Lesson #36: There's Never a Reason for Someone to Lose – The best scenarios occur when all parties can take away some value. If you can consistently create such scenarios, and people know you can create them, they come back for more. Many people returned to the pizza stand with stories of how my grandmother or grandfather – or both together – had helped them at some point in the past. And they usually brought all their family and friends to introduce them – perhaps even showcase them. And they always bought pizza.

Lesson #37: Reciprocity Works – And, even if it doesn't, trying to encourage it by first helping someone else leaves a good feeling inside. Towards the end of her life, my grandmother couldn't come to the Fair. She was sick in the hospital. Everyone wondered where she was. Well, word got out and soon my grandmother's hospital room was filled with cards, letters, flowers – you name it – all symbols of good tidings and good friends. These were not from her regular group of friends, but from vendors, suppliers, officials, and all sorts of Fair participants. My grandfather even arranged to have the disc jockey from WBEN call her in her hospital room, live, on the air, so she could speak to all her well-wishers. You can only imagine how good – how proud – this made her and our entire family feel.

Lesson #38: You Get More with Honey than You Get with Vinegar – This was one of my grandmother's favorite sayings. Whenever she overheard my brother and me talking about how to make sure someone doesn't take advantage of us, she'd say this. It's like what I wrote earlier, if you want something from someone, first find out what they want, and then find out how to get it for them. That's the essence of win-win. I perfected this at college to the point that, when they weren't calling me "Captain Chris" they were calling me "Don Carosa." Following my grandparents example, I tried my best to connect people with the things they wanted. My price back then? "Some day – and I hoped the day would never come – I would call upon them to return the favor..." No. Just kidding. I never actually said that or even implied it. Funny thing, though. The people I helped more often than not always happened to be there to return the favor.

You might think "win-win" means you have to give something up you don't want to give up. You might think "win-win" means you lose – you don't get what you want. You might think all of this and you'd be wrong. The "win-win" attitude is the cornerstone of successful selling. Consider this, when you buy something, you don't really care about all those bells and whistles, you only care about the bells and whistles that do something for you. You care only about what benefits you, not what features a particular product has. All good salesmen know this. They want to you "win" by benefiting from their product or service. In turn, they'll win when you make the purchase from them. These are just one of the tricks employed by those at the top of the sales game. You'll learn others in the next chapter.

20. THE ART OF THE SALE

No one has ever confused me with a salesman. Neither have I. I've never considered myself a salesman. I'm talking the door-to-door kind – the kind that can sit down one-on-one with you and get you to sign on the dotted line. I've seen really good salesmen who can do this and, I can tell you, I'm not one of them. But I get by. I am, however, very comfortable (and some have said quite good) at speaking to audiences – the larger the better. Long ago I realized my strengths and shortcomings pertaining to sales ability. I've learned to place myself in positions I can excel at, and rely on other people who are better in positions I'm less able to do.

Nonetheless, every business book needs to address this vital question: Why do customers buy and what do salesmen do to stoke that fire? Between working in the pizza stand and walking by – and watching – all those successful carnival barkers, I picked up on what I call "The Six Rules of a Good Carny." Here they are:

Rule 1: A good carny can sell snow to an Eskimo. (or, if not an Eskimo, then to someone from the snowbelts south of the City). These folks are masters of their craft. They've got the voice, they've got the manner, and they've got the instinct. I don't know if there's a "Carny School" they all go to, but they all share the same traits. It also makes you wonder, if you can't sell, can you still be a carny?

Rule 2: A good carny doesn't try to sell until he knows who his audience is. A good carny tailors his pitch to his audience. He keeps his pitch in his pocket and makes enough small talk to gauge the attitudes, convictions, and demeanor of the people around him. First, it's important to know there are two types of audiences. The distinction probably applies to most businesses, not just retail businesses like we have at the Fair. Here are the two types of audiences:

The Ephemeral Audience. They're the ones walking quickly by. You don't have time for an extensive dissertation. You've got to go rapid-fire with your best stuff. This means you only have time for a quick sound-bite. You choose a slogan and use it repeatedly. At the pizza stand, one of our favorites was "Pizza – it's Delicious and Nutritious." Better yet, pick a few slogans, just in case you've got slow strollers passing by the stand. Here are two others that proved effective for us: "Pizza! Hot Pizza! Right Out of the Oven!" and "Pepsi Here! Ice Cold Pepsi Here!" Of course, the ultimate "better yet" is try to catch the eye of the passerby and ask for the sale directly. We liked to ask, "Can You Smell that Delicious Home Made Pizza?" or "Is Your Wife Hungry for a Slice of Hot Pizza? Or "How about a refreshing Ice Cold Pepsi on this Hot Summer Day?"

The Captive Audience. This usually requires more of a deliberate slow-paced presentation. This methodical demonstration offers the classic overview of features and benefits. You have time to explore the prospect's obstacles and test ways to overcome them. At some point, you almost always have to ask for the sale. At the Fair, there are times when you want to extend the purchase process. Believe it or not, this activity actually attracts attention. People want to know what other people are buying. The bigger the ticket on the item, the more attention it will attract. Even with a captive audience, you always want to keep attracting more people.

Rule #3: A good carny instantly recognizes good prospects. Obviously, during rush times, you've got people who don't need convincing. They've already decided to make a purchase. Let them. In the case of a rush, they'll come knocking on your door (or up to the front of the stand). Your job is to not ask questions. Just process the order and move on. Don't try to sell them. Don't say anything except "How many slices would you like" and "That will be …" whatever the cost of those slices are. And you process those orders as fast as possible so potential customers don't walk away. Remember this: They will walk away if you look too busy.

Rule #4: A good carny quickly pushes aside bad prospects. Whether they're just walking past or sitting in front of you, some people are just never going to buy. Unless you're really, really, desperate (and despite what you may think, you're never that desperate), let them go. Move right on to the next person. Interesting, isn't it? In two of the three Rules I just covered (this one and the one above), a good carny keeps his mouth shut.

Rule #5: A good carny shares his secrets with other good carnies… but keeps the best ones to himself. Remember the power of reciprocity. The only way to get someone else's secrets is to give him a few of your own. But don't give away the entire store. Recall how I said I discovered six rules of a good carny? This list only contains five. Now you know why.

This might be a good time for the story of the cigarette lighters. It involves a lot of the elements of this chapter as well as some of the other chapters. One late afternoon, before dinner, we were preparing for a big rush. There was a major headliner in the grandstand that night and we knew there'd be a lot of people for dinner and a lot of people after the fireworks. My aunt and all my uncles came to help. That's how big a deal it was.

Just as the dinner rush was beginning – earlier than expected – one of my uncles came in happy as a clam. He was carrying a cardboard display of cigarette lighters. Upon entering the stand, he proudly proclaimed, "look what I got! It only cost me a dollar and we can easily sell them for a buck a piece!"

In my uncle's mind, that yielded a tidy profit of nearly $30. In my grandfather's mind, that meant my uncle was wasting time when he could have been helping at the stand. Remember, at this point, the expected rush was already underway. What happened next was the equivalent of striking one of those cigarette lighters in a barrel full of gun powder. Grandpa lit into my uncle in no uncertain terms. The roar must have been heard all the way into the grandstand, because, when my grandfather stopped yelling there was complete silence. I mean complete. My uncle didn't speak. My grandmother didn't speak. No one in the stand spoke. None of the customers spoke, either – and they were three-deep by this point.

We just quietly served. It was a rush, after all. No talking, just processing orders. Quick in, quick out. And the customers kept coming, like the Persians descending on the 300 Spartans at Thermopylae. (No, wise guys, this was not part of the Peloponnesian War – that was a little later – but thanks for remembering.) The hordes kept coming and coming.

And then they stopped. The show was starting.

But no sooner had we gathered our senses – and determined exactly how many more pizzas we could sell – the masses returned. The show was over. Pizza in. Pizza out. It didn't stop. And people wanted the pizza now!

And then we simply ran out. We had used up all the pizza shells we had. We were processing orders so fast, everyone was working so hard, that we forgot to pay attention to our inventory. My grandfather dispatched one of my uncles (not the one who brought in those ill-fated lighters, but another one) to go to a competitor to get more shells. We told the crowd it would be only a few minutes.

But a hungry crowd is an angry crowd. And an angry crowd is an unruly crowd. And the pizza stand is only made out of flimsy plywood. My grandfather knew all this and sensed the need to do something.

And he did.

He bolted from the rear of the stand and grabbed the cardboard display of cigarette lighters. He swooned to the front of the stand – in front of this crazed crowd – like Frank Sinatra in front of so many bobbysoxers. And then he poured it on like only he could. (Recall he was the personality of the stand and the pizza personality of the Fair.) The crowd cowed with respect as he began – to sell the cigarette lighters! My brother and I stood there in disbelief not so much that he was selling the lighters, but that he was selling the lighters like Moses coming down from Mount Sinai with the Ten Commandments. Only my grandfather didn't have the Ten Commandments, he had a cardboard display of about thirty cigarette lighters.

But, noooo! These were no mere cigarette lighters. These were "special" never before available (from our pizza stand) cigarette lighters. My grandfather didn't make anything up. He was reading mostly from the description on the cardboard display. But the way he was saying it, well, that made all the difference to the crowd. They bought him. They bought his pitch. And they bought the lighters – not for the one dollar my uncle suggested, but for two and three dollars apiece! With the audience warmed up, he turned the cardboard display over to my uncle who had originally brought them. My uncle sold the rest, copying exactly what his father had showed him. The rest of us took pre-orders for the pizza that would soon be there.

We ended up grossing probably a hundred dollars on that silly little cardboard display with the cigarette lighters. Heck, my uncle even got someone to buy the cardboard display when he ran out of lighters. My other uncle came with the extra shells. We filled all the pre-sale orders and eventually sold out of all those shells, too, but not before everyone who wanted some got their pizza.

Lesson #39: Successful Selling Begins with a Winning Process, Not a Smiling Personality – When I began working in the pizza stand, I can't say I had much of a personality. Quite the contrary, many would say I had an affection for scientific (some would say "anal") thinking. In fact, people signed my high school year book "To Mr. Spock." Because I recognized selling was just a system, I was therefore predisposed to pick up and quickly put into practice the sales process that worked so well for successful carnies like my grandfather. During my tenure at the Fair, I developed my sales personality by watching the best carnies – and, especially, my grandfather – throughout the fair. By the time I was a sophomore in college, in a riff off of "Captain Kirk," my classmates referred to me as "Captain Chris."

Lesson #40: Go After Low Hanging Fruit – Have you noticed the amount of paragraphs in this book I've devote to the various rushes during the day? What are some of the traits of a rush? The lines are long. We don't have to market the pizza. We just have to take orders. Nobody ever tries to pay less or even questions the price. Everybody just cares about buying the food, so they don't want to slow you down by talking to you. Once the sale is complete, they don't stay and chit-chat, they make for the nearest clear spot in the shade and eat. The customers are self-regulating, meaning they funnel through the front of the stand like an automated assembly line.

This can only lead us to one conclusion: A customer is willing to pay more when he's hungry. As we've seen, they're even willing to pay more for something they can't eat – cigarette lighters. This conclusion has a corollary: A customer is willing to pay more when he's thirsty. All in all, thirsty or hungry, these are the best customers to have.

Lesson #41: Never Underestimate Good Marketing (No Matter How Great the Product, the Sizzle Creates the Sales) – We like to think our pizza would sell itself, but that's exactly what every other pizza vendor at the Fair thought. It's not like we were trying to drive any of the other stands out of business by outselling them. We each had our own natural "territory" (it seemed as if the Fair Committee made sure we were evenly spaced). As a result, we all got a decent amount of sales, each pizza vendor selling enough pizza to keep wanting to come back to the Fair the next year. So, we didn't really compete against them, we competed against ourselves.

Given our location, we could expect a consistent amount of sales. We wanted to sell beyond our expectations. Any product, no matter how good, will sit on the shelves if no one knows it's there. Our job – those of us assigned to the front of the stand – was to make sure people knew about our pizza. We made sure they knew the moment a new pizza came out of the oven. We made sure they knew precisely how many fresh slices were left. We made sure they knew exactly when the next sizzling hot pizza would emerge from the oven. And, yes, we weren't afraid to use the word "sizzling" to sell our pizza.

Again, despite what Lesson #39 says, personality will sell. It sells radio shows. It sells television shows. It wins elections. It wins beauty contests. And it sells pizzas (and cigarette lighters if we run out of pizza).

Lesson #42: Never Underestimate Good Engineering (No Matter How Good the Promotion, the Product is What Keeps Them Coming Back) – Sure, our marketing was goofy, entertaining, and enjoyable for all those involved. What kept them coming back for more, however, wasn't the oversized novelty sunglasses. It was the sight of the fresh baked pizza. It was the sound of the oven door opening and shutting, meaning real pizza was being cooked by real Italians. It was the consistency of the product. My brother's job – and all those who worked in the back – was to make sure every pizza looked, smelled, and tasted just like every other pizza. My job – and everyone who worked in the front – was to make sure we cut the pizza so every slice was the same size. But most of all, it was the sweet smell of my grandfather's home-made pizza sauce.

There were many shared jobs in the pizza stand. Even the wearing of the oversized novelty sunglasses was shared between my grandfather and me. But there was one job only one person did. That was to make the sauce. Only my grandfather was permitted to do that. I'm sure my grandmother could have done it and I know my uncles and my mother and my aunt could have done it, but none of them dared to cross that line. My grandfather did allow my brother to "help." And by "help" I mean, "Kenny, get me this" and "Kenny, get me that." The making of the sauce occurred in secret behind the pizza stand. To this day, that recipe remains a secret – known only to the family now four generations removed from its initial use.

Selling is an involved process, but, when you strip it to its bare essentials, it's a very simple process. That doesn't mean everyone can do it. It just means everyone should be able to explain it. It's based on this one plain maxim: Everything has its price. If you're trying to buy something, this means there's a price at which someone is willing to sell an item to you. If you're trying to sell something, this means there's a price at which someone is willing to buy an item from you. It's only money. Money is a commodity. There are always ways to get more. Plus, no one ever argues over the value of money. It's worth the same for everyone. That's why it's so easy for anyone to describe the selling process. But there's another form of commerce that doesn't involve money. Not only is it much more difficult to describe than selling, it's a lot harder to do. Even great salesmen find it a challenge. What is it? And why is it important for you to master it? The answers begin on the next page.

21. THE ART OF THE DEAL

There was never any question of Grandpa's deal-making prowess nor of his deal-making prerogative. He owned the stand. It was his money that paid for the inventory. Therefore, he could do anything he wanted to with it. He had been making deals so long by the time Kenny and I had arrived on the scene that all he needed to do was to nod his head in a certain way and the deal would be done. Most of his deals weren't outright deals at all. They were reciprocating actions – the "You rub my back I'll rub yours" kind. There was never a hand shake. There was never a verbal acknowledgement. There was always, though, an enduring friendship that sealed the tacit deal.

I could never do one of those. I wasn't on the scene long enough to make those kinds of lasting friendships. I wish I could have, but, I really think those kinds of relationships can only exist between the pros. My grandparents were the pros. They owned the stand. Everyone knew they called the shots. If someone ever wanted something done pertaining to the stand, they knew only my grandparents could pull the trigger.

Still, I set myself up as a modest deal-maker. I did it partly for the challenge – the same way my grandfather played cards – and partly for Kenny's entertainment. He was always egging me on to make "a bigger trade." Like I said before, he was the expert at finding the freebies. When something he wanted wasn't a freebie, that's when he called me in. Sometimes I could trade for it, sometimes I couldn't. But it was all small-time stuff – in the beginning.

I started by trading slices that normally couldn't be sold. They were either cut too small or they just didn't look as appetizing. The first thing we'd normally consider doing was eating these slices. And when I say "we" I mean all the people in the stand – my grandparents included. At first, if we weren't hungry enough to eat them, I'd ask my grandmother if I could offer them for trade. Since she couldn't think of any other use for them, she had no problem saying "yes."

My grandfather, on the other hand, put his foot down when he found out. Once he did that, my grandmother was more hesitant to say yes. But I always found a way to convince her. And the best time to convince her was to wait for my grandfather to go off on one of his little treks. In a way, that's also how I graduated from small-time trader to medium-time trader. I still couldn't snag the big game, but I had moved up from bargaining for the trinkets Kenny found to trading for food. These kinds of trades my grandmother could swallow – literally. And she often benefited from the trade. She particularly enjoyed the French fries from the trailer two positions to the east of ours.

One time we ended up with a little bit too much food. We couldn't eat it all before my grandfather returned. He saw it sitting there and wanted to know who bought it. Kenny, afraid we'd be accused of spending money on something we shouldn't have, said no one bought it. Well, this sure sparked my grandfather's curiosity and I eventually had to fess up. Boy did Grandpa yell at me. "What right did you have to trade my pizza!" "If I ever catch you trading again, you'll have to pay for the pizza!" And so on and so forth. I'm sure my grandmother would have defended me, but her mouth was full of that very same food I had just traded for.

So, after a few seconds of pregnant silence following my grandfather's tirade, Kenny asked of the contraband food, "Since no one else wants it, can I eat it?"

"No!" Grandpa snaps back. "Since it was paid for with my pizza, it's my food." And he gulped it down.

As he left the stand, I could have sworn he said to my grandmother, "Hey, that tasted pretty good. Make sure he gets more next time."

This continued throughout my years working in the stand, Kenny daring me on to bigger ticket items and me gladly accepting the taunt. My grandmother tried her best to look away, partly to avoid the appearance of approving our furtive dealing, but mostly to warn us if she saw my grandfather returning.

Like I said, I didn't always get what I wanted. On the flip-side, I didn't always trade when someone else wanted to. By my later years, I was in the big-time. People were coming to me offering trades. We had a popular product. People wanted our pizza, especially people who worked at the Fair. They came from all corners offering items I could buy for less than the cost of the pizza they wanted. They knew that, but they hoped I didn't know that. They quickly discovered I did know. I turned a lot of these people down, sometimes because I just wasn't interested in the trade, sometimes because my grandfather was around.

Many of these carnies tried to trade with items they were otherwise giving away for free at their stand. Kenny instantly knew that, and he'd chime in for me "Why would he trade a slice for that if he can get it for free?"

It just so happens those were the exact circumstances that led to my second-greatest trade. One afternoon a young guy maybe a little older than us came by seeking to trade for a couple slices of pizza. He was working for a radio station. His job was to bring in the merchandise they were giving away for free. Every day it was something different. On that particular day, it was little blue jugs of Dynamo – a concentrated form of laundry detergent. Kenny had already gotten a free one for me and him. The guy offered to trade a jug for a couple slices of pizza.

"No way," I said. "The pizza is worth way more than that jug. Plus, those things are free. We already have two of them."

But the guy was hungry and desperate. He said he could get me an entire case (with 24 bottles in it) for two slices of pizza.

I paused and looked around. My grandfather was there. I told the guy, "OK, but I have to bring the pizza to you. I can't let my grandfather see me trading."

The guy agreed and told me he'd be in the grandstand where the radio station was. About a half hour later, I grabbed two of those not-so-perfect slices I referred to before and told Kenny, "I'm going to walk around to the front of the stand. You hand these to me." I did that and headed for the grandstand with the two slices.

Inside, there was a huge line at this radio station. Everybody wanted their little blue jug of Dynamo! I asked for the guy and he appeared. I offered him the two slices of pizza and asked for my case in return. Now it was his turn to be afraid of being seen trading. "I can't give it to you here in front of all these people. I'll have to bring it to the stand."

"In which case," I said, withdrawing the two slices, "I'll have to hold on to these." And I walked back to the stand.

A few minutes later I saw the guy pulling a hand truck with eight cases of Dynamo on it. I figured one of those were mine. Nope. The guy came up to me and said he wanted a whole pie for the eight cases. I replied, "I can't do that. All I can give you are these two slices." They were the same slices I had brought to the grandstand. By now, they were very cold.

The guy, obviously very hungry and apparently with no cash, pleaded with me. But I held my ground. Finally, his sad face got the best of me, so I said, "How about if I throw in a nice cold glass of Pepsi?" I knew this would not cost us anything because I was going to use one of those infamous "no-charge" cups.

The fraught guy quickly agreed. He brought the cases in the back and came around for the pizza and pop. To show him what a nice guy I am, I offered to heat up the slices. But he was too hungry and declined the offer.

He snatched the slices from me and gobbled them down. Then he trotted off to the grandstand, never to be seen again.

In the meantime, my grandmother wanted to know what all the cases of Dynamo were for. By now, I was beginning to feel like Milo Minderbinder from *Catch-22*. I had just made this great trade and I didn't know what to do with it. At most, I needed one case. I told my grandmother I'd give the rest to her and my mother.

Just then my grandfather came back. Now it was his turn to ask what these cases of Dynamo were doing there. I couldn't hold back. I figured even *he* would be proud of my trade. So I started to tell him I traded for them.

He immediately cut me off. He was really mad. He couldn't believe how selfish and greedy I was. He wanted to know what I was going to do with all these cases, anyway?

Just then my grandmother interrupted. "Chris," she said, "tell your grandfather what you just told me."

And I did. And that changed my grandfather's tune. "You mean, you were going to give these seven cases to your mother and grandmother all along?"

"No," I said honestly. "The original trade was for only one case. Two slices for a case. I was going to take a few bottles and give the rest to Grandma and my mother. But then the guy brings eight cases and asks for more. He wanted a whole pie."

"Oh," said my grandfather, expecting the other shoe to drop. "So you had to give him more than two slices for the eight cases?"

"Well it was only fair," I said. "I gave him a Pepsi – in a no-charge cup."

"Wait," said my grandfather in disbelief. "For these eight cases, all you gave this guy was two slices of pizza and a Pepsi – in a no-charge cup?"

"Yep."

My grandfather paused, looked at the eight cases, then looked at me. "That was a pretty good deal." And then he went on with his business.

He never bothered me again about trading.

Except for once.

Remember that electric frying pan from the I-Got-It! game my grandmother always wanted? One evening on the last day of the Fair, my grandfather summoned me over. In a hushed voice, so my grandmother couldn't here, he said to me, "Chris, you know that electric frying pan at the I-Got-It! game your grandmother always wanted? I want to surprise her with it. Think you can make a deal for it?"

Wow. This was the pro asking me to the Big Leagues. I couldn't believe it. With pride gushing through my veins, I coolly said, "Yes." and proceeded to lay out the strategy for getting it.

That night, my grandfather surprised my grandmother with the new electric frying pan. She was so happy she stood up on her tippy toes, gave my grandfather a big hug (which was really tough for her on account of him being so much bigger than her), and gave him a big kiss.

That was my greatest trade ever.

Lesson #43: There's a Time to Sell and There's a Time to Barter – Know the difference. The first important thing you have to know is the liquid value of the properties being traded. This isn't the asking price. It's the actual price some objective buyer is willing to pay for the item. This is often a lot less than the asking price. Sometimes, it's better just to sell them the pizza rather than trying to make a trade.

Lesson #44: Remember the Lesson of Win-Win – They won't come back if they think you're out to take advantage of them. I started as a small-time trader and had to work my way up to the Big Leagues. This meant making a lot of people win on the way up. And I kept them winning. The only way people will want to deal with you is if you are fair, honest, and always leave something on the table for them. If you constantly beat them to the ground, there's no incentive for them to come back, which leads to this last lesson...

Lesson #45: Honesty is the Best Policy – A small deal today will lead to a big deal tomorrow. This is just like the lesson of working hard. You need to work hard to make sure a deal is fair to everyone. In fact, it's probably a good idea to give the other guy a meaningful victory every now and then. This way, sometime in the future when the deal means a lot more to you than to him, maybe he'll cut you a break.

Humility, staying cool, creating win-win scenarios, selling, and dealing, these are all important aspects of running a business. They all, however, represent only the tactical aspects of business. Successful businesses don't just employ tactics, they carry out broader strategies. I won't get into the morass of how to create a strategic plan. There are plenty of others who have already done a very good job at explaining how to do that. Instead, the next chapter will explore some of the less talked about elements of the strategic process. It's less about planning and, in keeping with my grandfather's style, more about the practical implementation of that strategy.

22. THE ART OF BUSINESS

If you're familiar with the Taoist concept of Yin and Yang, you'll know the concept of how opposing forces, indivisible and permanent, contain synergies that make the whole greater. Business is like that. On one hand you have the idea of business being all about blocking and tackling. In this sense, no matter how good the idea, it's the basic and boring details that make a business successful. On the other hand, business thrives on innovation (or, as we liked to say in the pizza stand, "Always think outside the pizza box"). A business that isn't constantly growing in new and different ways is dying in the routine of same-old-same-old.

The pizza stand resembles this Yin and Yang concept perfectly. In terms of blocking and tackling, my grandparents had it down – and they made sure my brother and I also had it down, at least for our limited roles. But my grandparents' roles weren't limited. Together, they covered the entire business. My grandfather was a whiz at making pizza. My grandfather was a whiz at selling pizza. My grandfather was a whiz at making friends.

But it was my grandmother who made the business successful. She kept track of all the money during the day. My grandfather knew his limitations: He could flawlessly mix the elements of the recipe of his home-made pizza sauce but there were certain things he knew were best for him to delegate. Same thing when it came to government relations. My grandmother took care of that (e.g., she dealt with the "tax" men). My grandfather either knew these kinds of people could intimidate him, or (and more likely), in the still sexist world which we lived, my grandfather knew a woman (in this case my grandmother) could more easily manipulate the authorities than could a man. Finally, my grandmother had the job of recounting all the money at the end of the night. When she was done counting it, she hid it. Though he'd deny it, she honestly believed my grandfather had a propensity of spending loose cash.

Opposite of this steady-as-she-goes routine is the idea of invention and continual improvement. My grandparents best exemplified this when it came to starting the original pizzeria in Blasdell. This included their initial entrée into the Fair. They experimented by coming to the Fair to plug their brick and mortar business. They soon discovered the Fair business could stand on its own. Once at the Fair, they rapidly moved from a tent-based food booth in a larger food court to an independent pizza stand. And that creative thinking didn't stop there. You know those food trucks so popular in downtown city streets today? Well, my grandfather had the idea of a traveling pizza truck. Just like the ice cream man comes ringing in suburban neighborhoods, so, too, once did my grandfather come ringing in those same neighborhoods with his pizza truck.

Along these same lines comes a story involving me and my brother. It didn't take me long to notice the customers often specifically asked for the pizza with the most pepperoni. Conversely, they complained about paying the same for a slice with fewer pepperoni slices. I brought this up to Kenny and showed him what usually happened to the pepperoni when I cut the pies. He came up with a new idea on how to assemble the pizza. By accounting for the way I cut it, he figured out a way to make sure each slice had two pieces of pepperoni on it. We figured this out during one afternoon lull and Kenny prepared about a half dozen pizza pies in this fashion.

My grandparents had been away from the stand during all this. When they came back, they took one look at Kenny's new assembly method and gave it a thumbs down. Once again, as with the "short-cut" lesson that led to the story about the Irish Neighborhood, my grandparents questioned why we were changing the ways they had been doing things. The pizza, with its pepperoni now perfectly placed, no longer looked like a homemade pizza. It looked like one of those frozen pizzas you buy at the grocery. Our attempts to explain our logic fell on deaf ears. Fortunately, they let Kenny keep the pizzas he had previously assembled under this new method.

This gave us the opportunity to show them the result of our idea. We cooked those pizzas, I cut them and each identically-sized slice had the identical number of pepperoni on it. Every slice looked the same. People no longer wasted our time requesting a particular slice. People no longer complained about getting too few pepperoni. In short, the plan worked precisely as expected. The assembled pizza might have looked like a store-bought pizza, but we sold it by the slice, not by the pie. Customers didn't care what the pie looked like, they cared about what the slices looked like.

Then my aunt and uncles came to help in the dinner rush. When they saw how Kenny made the pizzas, they complained just like my grandparents did. Only, this time, it wasn't me and Kenny explaining why we did this, it was my grandparents. Having seen our plan in practice, they recited all the reasons we had previously given.

Like I said, my grandparents believed you need to work hard to succeed and that usually meant not taking short-cuts and doing the same thing over and over again. At the same time, they embraced innovation. They knew the business' survival demanded they keep up with the latest trends, wants, and needs of the markets they served.

Lesson #46: Know What You're Good At and Know What the Other Guy Must be Good At – And concentrate on that. This is the blocking and tackling side of the equation. Even in a small business, the division of labor is critical. Entrepreneurs most often fail because they insist on continuing to perform all functions. Those start-up businesses that go on to survive through the ten-year mark have owners who understand what they do best and who hire other people to do the other things.

Lesson #47: Structure is Fine, But Always Think Outside of the Pizza Box – You never know where the next great idea will come from. If you're the entrepreneur, don't be afraid to try something new that your staff comes up with. That being said, you better also be sure you know how to judge the effectiveness of these new ideas. Are they truly making your internal processes more effective – or are they mere short-cuts leading you into unknown territory.

Lesson #48: Always Have a Plan C – Because you never know when Plan B will fail. Once, the gas line feeding the pizza oven went dead. It was a Fair-wide problem not limited to our stand. My grandfather had a contingency plan in case this happened. He had a spare tank of propane just for this purpose. He called one of my uncles and asked him to bring the propane to the Fair. He called my other uncle and asked him to do something else. The uncle came with the propane. They tried to hook it up, but it didn't work. That was Plan B. A very short while later, my other uncle showed up with two electric pizza ovens from the Pizzeria. We immediately plugged those in and started cooking pizza right away. That was Plan C.

So there you have it. Or do you? I've laid out all the pieces of the puzzle for you. There's only one thing left to do…

PART V

LIFE'S LAUNCHING PAD

– A Never Ending Battle –

23. PUTTING IT ALL TOGETHER

It was the summer of 1981. I was about to become a college senior. Graduation was less than a year away. I was on top of the world. By the end of my junior year, I had already begun to put some of these lessons into action. As I mentioned earlier, my brother and I had a small sports card "business." I say "business" because we were never in it for the money. We were in it to expand our collections. Our total income could have been counted in the hundreds of dollars. We started that business in high school, so our ambitions were perhaps a bit muted.

Sophomore year in college I wanted to become a "player" in the realm of politics. This was no easy task for a Physics and Astronomy major swarmed by a sea of Political Science and Economics majors. They all knew far more about political theory and practice than I did. I could only learn from them (and I did), but what I really wanted to do was to lead them. I narrowed my strategic advantage down to one subject: Math. (Are you detecting a trend here?) I may not have been able to hold my own in a debate of the various "isms" of Poly Sci, but when it came to interpreting numbers, no one could beat me. The art of politics intersects with the science of mathematics at the corner of polling and human behavior. This psychological flavor of the numbers gave me a further edge. I started a business called "Student Polling Services." I brought together underclassmen and we did telephone-based market research, initially for presidential campaigns prior to the Connecticut primary, but then for local candidates. We eventually conducted market research for commercial enterprises. I used all the tricks I learned about selling (I once held back on results until a politician's check cleared) and dealing (one campaign paid me in baseball cards). This business grossed a few thousands of dollars.

But the biggest coup was my radio station experience. I had been an AM disk jockey, eventually becoming the station's most listened to on-air personality by playing oldies requests. At the same time, I was manager of the hockey team. I noticed there were a lot of local fans – not just college students – and we continually played before sell-out crowds. Now, unlike most hockey managers – who did everything themselves – I accumulated a staff of willing and able classmates to do all the work during game nights. I was a miniature version of my grandfather, roaming the rink glad-handing people, a (very) minor celebrity of sorts. Thinking outside the box quickly upgraded that minor to major. I convinced my radio station to allow me to restart its decades dormant sports broadcasting arm. With a box full of electronic equipment, I instantly became technical director, producer, play-by-play announcer and chief salesman for a fledging Division I college sports broadcasting department. The only thing I didn't do was color, and I made sure to carefully select well-known college students (i.e., those who by themselves would draw listeners) to fill that role. This little venture grossed the nearly bankrupt station tens of thousands of dollars. I, of course, was more than happy enough to accept my 20% commission.

So, as I said, heading into the Fair that summer I was on top of the world. I was about as BMOC at school as a non-athlete could be. I knew the Fair like the back of my hand. The Dynamo trade had established my "Carny-hood" of sorts. Was there anything I couldn't do?

Yes.

Each day, a particularly pretty girl would walk by the stand. She occasionally stopped to ask my grandparents how everything was going. She was my age and was working as a vendor liaison for the Fair Committee. This was a fairly prestigious position for a college student, and she walked proudly, wearing this honor on the chip of her shoulder.

But she was pretty. My grandmother noticed I had a habit of eying her. Kenny noticed too. One day, he dared me to really talk to her. Not about business, and not about going out on a date, but enough so that she would notice me. That's what his words said. What he really meant was, "I bet you can't get her to let you visit her at her college." I smelled the challenge and one-upped him. I bragged I could get her to invite me to her room (but that was all – my intentions were definitely G rated).

We waited for her daily stroll. When she walked by, I shouted, "Hey! What school do you go to?" She replied, her nose firmly pointing to the sky, "Cornell" without breaking her pace.

Several times I tried to get her to talk as she walked past. Several times she snubbed me and continued to walk by. I began to call her "Cornell" in a familiar way in an attempt to lower her defenses. That didn't work, either.

Finally, she had to stop by on official business. My grandmother stayed in the back of the stand, forcing her to get her daily check-up answers from me.

Throughout the professional conversation, I could really detect a very blatant snobbish attitude. She knew she was an Ivy League prodigy. To her, I was just a carny. Sensing this, I set her up. I asked her again if she really went to Cornell. She confirmed it, again with her nose in the air. I jokingly said, "That's OK, I'll still talk to you. It may not be Yale, but it's still Ivy."

She did a double-take. He eyes told me she couldn't believe a Yale man would agree to work such a lowly job. Anticipating her question, I told her, "This is my grandparents' pizza stand, and I wouldn't trade this job for any other job at the Fair."

It was immediately clear she thought I was higher on the totem pole than she was. I didn't do anything to really merit this, but I was more than willing to go along with it. She told me everything about her, from her major to her sorority. Somehow, I let it "slip" I was the sports director for a small New Haven radio station. I told her we'd be going to Cornell that fall to broadcast the Yale game. I further told her that I was wondering if she wouldn't mind if I interviewed her live on the air during half time. At that point, she was living her dream. Then, in the *coup de grace*, I told her that I was carrying very expensive equipment and, well, the place I was staying at wasn't very secure – you know, wild-college-party not secure. I asked, "Can I store my equipment overnight in your room at the sorority?" She readily agreed, and whirled away on to her next stop, a slight lilt in her step.

My brother – totally quiet – stood next to me this whole time. When she left, he burst out laughing, not believing I had done what I had just done. I started laughing, too. I turned towards my ever-watchful grandmother. Certainly, she would be proud the way I turned the tables on this girl.

But her scowl said otherwise. Without her breathing a word, it had told me everything I needed to know. I had broken the rule of humility. I had needlessly dropped names like "Yale" and mentioned my position in a braggish way. Worse, I had unfairly used my God-given talents to take advantage of someone. Certainly, she hadn't raised her grandson to act the way I had acted.

Kenny and I abruptly stopped laughing. We turned away from my grandmother's gaze, tails between our legs, and went back to watching the people walk by.

Yes, I kept my word. I, somewhat more embarrassed now, feebly placed my equipment in her room – and promptly left. I interviewed her live on the air as promised and could tell it was the highlight of her college career. To me, being on the air was nothing but a job. But it was her dream-come-true, and I did nothing to shatter that dream. Before the start of the third quarter, I thanked her for all her help and waved goodbye. I never saw her again.

Lesson #49: The Importance of Learning by Doing – Imitation is more than a great form of flattery, it's a great form of learning. The Boy Scouts teach both adult leaders and young boys something called the EDGE method. It's really a business management technique. It stands for Educate, Demonstrate, Guide, and Enable. It's all about learning by doing. Long before I learned this fancy acronym, I learned how to do it by working in my grandparents' pizza stand at the Erie County Fair.

Lesson #50: The Importance of Self-Confidence – There are thousands of naysayers in your life, and, if you start your own business or come up with a novel idea for an existing business, you're sure to meet them all. There's only one thing that can defeat this army of "No's" – and that's self-confidence. In the course of learning by doing, you gradually gain the self-confidence of the routine. Once you've mastered the routine, you'll have the confidence to think outside the pizza box. I learned this firsthand by working in my grandparents' pizza stand at the Erie County Fair.

Lesson #51: The Importance of Deciding – Eventually, if you're going to amount to anything in this life, you've got to take the leap, you've got to decide. John F. Kennedy, paraphrasing Dante Alighieri, once said, "The hottest places in hell are reserved for those who, in times of great moral crisis, maintain their neutrality." It is the fear of failure that quells peoples' ability to make decisions. "This miserable way" – and now I'm actually quoting Dante, from *Inferno*, canto iii – "is taken by the sorry souls of those who lived without disgrace and without praise. They now commingle with the coward angels, the company of those who were not rebels nor faithful to their God, but stood apart. The heavens, that their beauty not be lessened, have cast them out, nor will deep Hell receive them - even the wicked cannot glory in them." The best decisions require not just keen analysis, but, and especially in times when analysis runs dry and you've got to go with your gut, extreme self-confidence. Sometimes the decision itself isn't perfect, but it is the will of self-confidence than makes that decision work. I discovered this by working in my grandparents' pizza stand at the Erie County Fair.

Lesson #52: The Importance of Failure – Fear of failure is the biggest obstacle to making decisions. To really learn by doing, in a self-confident manner, is to make a decision to act, and then see yourself fail. Thomas Edison, when asked about his many failed efforts to find a practical incandescent light bulb, famously said, "I have not failed. I've just found 10,000 ways that won't work." Before you can find the ways that work, sometimes you must find the ways that don't work. Don't be afraid to find those ways. Find them. Find them quickly. Then move on. I found this out by working in my grandparents' pizza stand at the Erie County Fair.

Lesson #53: The Importance of Success – Nothing motivates you more than the glory of success. But here's the key to success – it doesn't come from selling the whole pizza pie all at once, it comes from selling one slice at a time. Many management gurus emphasize the importance of not merely defining the big, hairy, audacious, goal. No. They instead demand you focus on the small steps on the critical path towards achieving that big, hairy, audacious, goal. Each small step represents a small victory. And each small victory represents a small success. And each small success excites you, nudging you ever so closer to that big success you've spent a lifetime trying to attain. Along the way on this journey, you may have a few regrets, you will bite off more than you can chew, and, as a result, you'll suffer your share of losing. In the end, though, as you stand atop that mountain, you'll look back and find it all so amusing.

There was one more lesson my grandparents taught me. This one didn't occur at the pizza stand. It happened in the most unlikely of places in the most unlikely of ways. It was the final lesson, the capstone of all the others.

EPILOGUE: THE CODA OF LIFE

(May, 1982)

I stood at the piano in the elegant Common Room of Yale University's Davenport College when I caught a glimpse of my family approaching in the grassy courtyard outside – my parents, my brother and sisters, and my mother's parents – my grandparents. Though my eyes grew excited my mind and my mouth didn't break from the mid-song lyrics of *My Way*. They entered the room just as we finished, but I knew they could hear me as they walked on the slate sidewalk towards the entrance. We had the windows fully open to let in the fresh sunny May air.

The impromptu lounge act came courtesy of a week-long celebration called Senior Week. It's a tradition of all graduating seniors. We let our inhibitions down in different ways. My roommate one night chose to ride his motorcycle through that very same Common Room I was in. That day, I chose to sing – something I hadn't done in earnest since elementary school (my singing at the pizza stand was more parody than anything else). That I chose Sinatra only made sense. My pride in my family's heritage was by then well known to my Yale classmates (remember, they called me "Don Carosa"). It was therefore a big honor for me to introduce my family to my friends. My friends were equally honored to be introduced, especially to my grandparents.

What impressed me most that day was my grandmother. I knew she had a serious case of cancer. I had thought her condition was growing worse every day. But, on the bright spring day in New Haven, she had the look of a carefree school girl – from her well groomed hair to her Sunday-best dress and her fur piece. It struck me. I knew she looked far better than she must have felt, but she showed no hint of her condition. In fact, her chipper disposition gave my classmates great pleasure to be around her.

I felt grateful she would put aside her own pain just to be with me on the day of my graduation from college. I was the oldest grandson, so I was a little used to sharing many firsts with my family. But I took a more business-like approach to my college graduation. I stayed cool, like it was no big deal, like I had been there before. To be honest, it wasn't like I dreamed of going to Yale all my life. It was just a happy accident. When my high school presented me with an assortment of college applications, I chose the one with my favorite color – blue. That it was "Yale" blue was a mere coincidence. Since the applications were stacked one on top of the other, I never saw the name of the schools. All I saw were the colors.

But my family, and especially my grandmother, refused to pretend it wasn't a big deal. That made me feel even better than I was already feeling.

The next day, it rained during the actual graduation, but my grandmother refused to stay in her hotel room. My grandfather wanted to. He had the same "cool" demeanor about the whole thing that I did. But – and I could to this day imagine my grandmother saying this: "Sam, we didn't come all this way just to stay in this room!" – my grandmother was adamant, she was going to participate in every single activity Yale would allow her to participate in.

And she did. Of all the events, it was the President's reception that sticks out the most. At the time, the President of Yale was A. Bartlett Giamatti (yes, his son Paul is the famous actor). Giamatti was of Italian heritage (the "A" stood for "Angelo"). I had always thought, as evidenced by the abandonment of his given first name "Angelo" for the more Anglo-Saxon middle name "Bart," he had forsaken his bloodline in exchange for Ivy League prestige. Still, he prided himself on being very approachable to everyone – students, faculty, staff, and, as was the case this day, the extended families of students.

There was a long line to meet Giamatti at the President's reception that day. It had stopped raining, but the day – and my grandfather – was still dreary. But not my grandmother. She was still wearing that same school girl look I saw a day earlier in the Davenport courtyard. Again, I knew she was trying to make sure that the day belonged to me and she wasn't going to let any of her personal problems spoil it. After an hour or so, it was finally our turn to shake Giamatti's hand. By that time, everyone was trying to speed through the line. Even Giamatti had dispensed with his usual small talk. I respected his time (and the time of the people behind me) by following this convention. I quickly shook his hand, made a polite comment, then introduced my parents and my siblings. As they passed through the line, I next introduced my grandparents – remember, both native Italians – to Giamatti. To my surprise, his eyes lit up, as though I had given him an opportunity he had long sought. He began talking in Italian with my grandparents. He spoke primarily with my grandmother.

The length of the conversation awed me. He could have merely said a polite "How do you do?" and went on to next family in line as he did with the countless families before us. Instead, he chose to engage in a good long conversation with my grandparents as if they were a couple of long lost paisans (don't forget, Giamatti didn't know me, and he certainly didn't know my grandparents).

Afterwards, I approached my grandmother. I just had to satisfy my curiosity. "So, what did you two talk about?" I inquired. "Chris," she began, her joyful smile still on her face, "you're not going to believe this, but the President of Yale University just spoke to me not just in Italian, but in my native dialect!"

I was, and will always be, forever impressed with A. Bartlett Giamatti.

$$*\qquad*\qquad*\qquad*\qquad*$$

About a year later, my grandmother passed away. We were all sad. We were all sad, especially my grandfather. But the show had to go on, and Kenny and I worked that year with my grandfather all the same. It wasn't the same. It wasn't the same for a lot of reasons, not just because my grandmother wasn't there. Kenny and I knew it was our time to move on. Like my aunt and uncles before us, it was our turn to focus on getting a career and starting a family. We didn't want to leave, but we knew we had to.

My grandfather instinctively knew it was time to hand over the reins of the stand. When he died a few years later, he knew the stand was in capable hands. A lot has changed since I worked there. Today, Salvator's Pizza Stand isn't a stand at all. In fulfilling my grandfather's dream to make the business a mobile business, it's now Salvatore's Pizza Trailer – prominently positioned right at the top of the Avenue of Flags.

Kenny went on to build a linear career, first as a housing inspector, then as a municipal building investigator, then as a home builder, then as a mortgage loan originator before finally expanding into the financial services industry. Each step built off the previous one, like so many layers of different pizza ingredients atop a foundation of fresh dough. Most important, just like he built the foundation of the pizza while working in the stand, Kenny designed and built all of the homes my parents and siblings live in, each one better than the previous. He's also married and has three children.

I'm married with three children, too. While my entrepreneurial spirit lay dormant, my intrepreneurial spirit flourished. In this company I helped create their mutual funds, transformed a back-office cost center into a strategic profit center, and started a trust company that grew to nearly one billion dollars in assets by the time I left. I left when I could no longer contain the entrepreneurial bug within me. In creating my own firm, I rediscovered much of what I had learned while working in that pizza stand at the Erie County Fair. But, best of all, as my grandmother had advised me, I got to share my

God-given talents for the benefit of other people. I still do it. The mission statement of my firm is "We Help People Achieve Their Lifetime Dreams."

I don't remember exactly why, but the subject of my college graduation had come up in a conversation with my mother. Perhaps I was feeling guilty that my grandmother had to travel seven hours from Buffalo to New Haven in her condition. While I was grateful she wanted to show how much she cared for me, I felt she didn't need to do it. I already knew she cared about me and everyone else in her family. I guess I was feeling really bad about the whole thing.

Then my mother said something that surprised me. "Chris," she said, "you've got it all wrong. Well, it's not that she didn't want to show you that she cared about it – she did – but that's not the reason she forced herself to go. You see, ever since she was a little girl, she wanted to go to Yale. She didn't dream of going to school there, she just wanted to visit the place. She was a teenager during the height of the roaring twenties, and there was this singer. His name was Rudy Vallee. He was the idol of all the teenage girls in her generation – your grandmother included. He's like Bing Crosby, Frank Sinatra, and the Beatles, only he was before them."

"Your grandmother would spend her days listening to Rudy Vallee sing about Yale, songs like "Boola Boola" and "The Whiffenpoof Song." She'd see pictures of him in his raccoon coat and read about his time going to school at Yale. For a young Italian immigrant, Yale seemed like a fairy tale land. She dreamt of one day going there, but she never did. She felt it was a goal beyond the reach for someone like her."

"Then, when you were a senior in high school, when she found out you got accepted to Yale, she couldn't contain herself. She was so happy. Right there, she vowed to go to your graduation, no matter what. I know she never told you about it, but you were making her dream come true."

"That's not the last of it. When the time came for you to graduate, she knew the cancer was bad, but she wasn't going to let that stop her for fulfilling her life-long dream. Remember how it rained the day of your graduation? She wasn't going to let that stop her from taking any time away from her walking in the same steps that Rudy Vallee did. But the biggest thing that happened was when she spoke with Bart Giamatti. There she was, a lowly immigrant girl, not just visiting Yale, but talking with the President of Yale – and he was speaking to her in her dialect! Of all the dreams she had, this went beyond them all!"

"And she realized those dreams all because of you."

Lesson #54: If You Learn the Right Lessons, Sometimes You Can Return a Favor in Ways You Never Imagined.

PART VI

APPENDIX

– Continuing Adventures –

APPENDIX I: BACK AT THE OLD PIZZA STAND

(excerpted from *50 Hidden Gems of Greater Western New York*)

In the early scene of the 1962 movie version of *The Music Man*, Harold Hill, con man extraordinaire, unexpectedly bumps into his old friend and accomplice Marcellus Washburn. Marcellus has since married a "nice comfortable girl" and settled down in the idyllic Midwestern town of River City ("Gone legitimate, huh? I knew you'd come to no good," laments Hill). When he asks Harold if he's still pitching steam automobiles, Hill shakes his head "No" and says, "I'm back at the old stand" whereupon he pantomimes conducting a band.

I can't say Hamburg had the stubbornness of River City, Iowa, (after all, Hamburg is the "Town that Friendship built"), but I can attest to an idyllic feeling growing up off South Park when it had only two lanes. And like the magical concluding scene of *The Music Man*, my brother and I (and maybe even my mother and father, too), couldn't wait to gaze in awe as the marching band led the parade down South Park to signal the beginning of the Big Tree Fireman's Carnival. We'd watch from the second floor apartment above my grandfather's pizza parlor across the street from Abbott Parkway where we lived. There was something dazzling about that marching band, and something incredibly comfortable about watching it from the large picture window overlooking the Avenue. There was also something indescribably exciting about that annual parade. It was an anticipatory pleasure for me and my brother, for we knew as soon as the parade ended, we would immediately head for the carnival.

But the carnival, while fun, only signaled the coming of something bigger: the annual Erie County Fair, or, as we (and many others) called it, the "Hamburg Fair." Funny thing about the two events, though. While the Big Tree Fireman's Carnival parade reminded me of *The Music Man*, the carnival did not. On the other hand, although the much larger Fair parade didn't evoke feelings of *The Music Man*, the fair itself oozed of River City. You might think *Meet Me In St. Louis* a better movie to compare to the Fair, and, for some, that may be true. For me, however, the sly con of Harold Hill and, much to his own surprise, his and River City's eventual transformation matched my own journey from boyhood to manhood, a journey that trekked through the Fair.

Before I get too involved in how the Fair helped shape my character, let's go back in time to the very beginnings of the Fair. Greater Western New York grew first as an agricultural region. It was (and some say it remains) colored more by the same soft brush of the Midwest farm belt rather than the spray painted tag of the urbanized East Coast. And if there's one American tradition best suited for farmers, it's the annual county fair. It seemed like every county in America's rich heartland held these yearly affairs and they became more than a social gathering of the local growers, but a showcase for the county and its people.

You might not know this, but the Erie County Fair is older than Erie County. The first Fair was held in October 1820 in the city of Buffalo on Main Street near the Terrace overlooking the waterfront.[1] In 1821, the very next year, Niagara County ceded its southern portion – including Buffalo – to create Erie County. The Fair's sponsoring organization – the Niagara County Agricultural Society was renamed the Erie County Agricultural Society to become the oldest civic, community member organization in Erie County.[2] The Society held a second Fair in 1821 but a poor economy and transportation logistics made continuing the Fair impractical.[3] The area's economy would soon change for the better as, on August 9, 1823, construction of the Buffalo end of the Erie Canal began.[4] By 1840, the Canal encouraged tens of thousands, some 40,000 in Erie County alone, to populate the westernmost section of the Holland Land Purchase.[5] In 1841, things had brightened up and, on October 5 and 6, the Erie County Fair started anew and has been held annually ever since (with the exception of 1943 as a result of World War II rationing).[6]

The success of the Fair received broad attention, and when New York State decided to hold its first State Fair in Buffalo in 1848, Robert McPherson, president of the Erie County Agricultural Society, said, "If the State of New York means to beat us in 1848, when they visit us, they must do their best."[7] In the early years, the City of Buffalo proved adequate as a location, but as the region grew, so, too, did the Fair. The Agricultural Society soon found it required a larger footprint than the City could provide, so in 1850 the Fair moved to Aurora.[8] After spending time in Lancaster, East Hamburgh (now Orchard Park) and West Seneca, it settled in Springville from 1851-1867.[9] In 1868, by a vote margin of but a single trustee, the board of the Erie County Agricultural Society approved a permanent move to its current location and, on September 23, 24 and 25, 1868, held its first County Fair in Hamburgh.[10] (By the way, it wasn't until 1877 that the Town decided to drop the second "h" in "Hamburgh." It is unknown if Pittsburgh picked up this superfluous h on waivers or not.) With the increase in publicity in the 1880s, the Erie County Fair quickly became known as "The Hamburg Fair." For example, in 1895 the Buffalo Courier wrote, "…not to have seen the Hamburg Fair… is to have missed one of the institutions in the vicinity of Buffalo."[11] Indeed, such was its success, a director of the Buffalo Pan-American Exposition committee, so frustrated by early proposals for that event, complained those drafts offered "a show of the size of the Hamburg Fair or the Toronto Exhibition."[12]

I still call it "The Hamburg Fair" and I expect many who grew up in Hamburg still proudly refer to it by that name. The Fair generated a lot of pride in our community and in our family. Historically larger even than the New York State Fair, in 1970 it became the country's largest county fair.[13] It has since slipped to the third largest county fair and, in that last decade or so, the New York State Fair has finally generated more visitors than the Erie County Fair (but just barely).

That the Fair is such a part of me and such a jewel in our community, I naturally assumed everyone felt the same way. But I'm constantly surprised, even to this day, when I find someone from the north towns of Buffalo who has never benefited from partaking of the Fair. Heck, there are people in Rochester who make the annual trek to the Erie County Fair! How could these Buffalonians forsake their own county's shining star?

Oh well, here's why the Fair became so important to me. Like the glamor of *The Music Man*, the Fair was one big show, with Hollywood entertainers often headlining the acts. It possessed a circus atmosphere – it even had (and still has) a Midway that arrived by train, just like an old circus. But there was one thing that made it most special to me and my family – it was a show that, since 1957, we were in!

You remember my grandfather's pizza parlor on South Park I mentioned earlier? It turns out my grandfather, although an entrepreneur – he once owned a grocery on Ridge Road in Lackawanna – only started the pizza parlor because my young mother nagged him. "Dad," she said one day in 1954, "it's the latest thing. All the kids are going. Besides, you can't make any money in the grocery business anymore, not with those big guys like A&P coming in." My grandfather, of course, reacted like any father would when his smart-aleck teenager tries to tell him what to do. I'm not saying there was a sonic boom on Ingham Avenue that day, but you get the picture. Apparently, he refused to believe anyone would order out something they could easily make at home. Still, by 1956, my grandfather had started the area's first pizza parlor, at least according to my mother. Now, I don't know how you reconcile "all the kids are going" with my mother's claim that it was the first pizza parlor in the area, but that's her story and she's sticking to it. There must be some truth to the story because, when word got around at the Lake-Erie Italian Club that Ilio DiPaolo wanted to start a pizzeria, my grandfather gladly gave Ilio the benefit of his experience.

Well, back in the old days, the Erie County – er – Hamburg – Fair had a tent where the local restaurateurs would set up to sell their culinary creations. It was there my grandparents first brought their pizza to sell to fairgoers. Soon, that makeshift booth beneath a shared tent became a free standing wooden stand across from the original main entrance to the grand stand at the top of the Avenue of Flags. That's where I remember hanging out as a little kid when I was too tired to tour the Fair or when my parents wanted to go see one of those Hollywood headliners. It's also where we'd escape from the crowd after witnessing the ultimate in coolness (for an eight-year-old at least) – like the Hell Drivers or Joey Chitwood's Thrill Show – or the ultimate in excitement – the massive demolition derby. Our neighbors always had a car in it. We cheered for them, but they never won.

Perhaps the greatest personal impact the Fair had on me occurred during the few years I worked there for my grandparents. Oh the stories I could tell. In fact, one of these days I might be inclined to pen a book along the lines of *Every Thing I Learned I Learned at the Hamburg Fair*. For the purposes of this book, though (and this chapter is already running too long), suffice it to say the Fair shares that quaintly all-American feel of the *The Music Man's* River City – for all its charm, all its lost innocence and all its carnival atmosphere. Judging from an Orange County (NY) reporter's account in the 1890s, "This Fair is unique among the County Fairs of the Empire State. First, it is well attended, and therefore successful financially; and, second, it can boast of being the most remarkable gathering of fakes on this earth...,"[14] since more than a century ago, the circus-like magic of *The Music Man* rings true.

Or at least it once did. Perhaps, in briefly calling itself "America's Fair" as it did in the 2000s to broaden its appeal, the Fair began trying too hard. The success of the Hamburg Raceway's Casino hasn't helped. The soft pebble gravel – that you once walked on, that once kicked up that country dust, that once coated your country sweat on those especially hot days – has long ago been replaced by the heartless hardness of asphalt. Yes, they paved paradise and made it a parking lot.

But they can make as many changes as they want. They can get rid of the double Ferris Wheel – which we could see from Highland Avenue on a clear day. They can get rid of the Sky Way that once flew above the Midway and, from which, much to the distress of those walking below, occasionally rained little red I-Got-It! balls. They can outlaw rickety wooden vendor stands and replace them with antiseptic Jetson-like trailers. They can even charge vendor rates so high the Boston Church can't sell enough pies to afford the rent.

They can do all that, but they can never remove the memories of River City. The memories where, for one week (or ten days) a year, I got to live the 20-hour work day life of a carny (my grandparents insured I never found out what they did the other eight hours). Or, the memories where, by working so closely with my grandparents, I received invaluable education about life, family and fun. Among these include showing unconditional love for their children despite yelling at them for the silliest reason, like the time my uncle showed up one afternoon with a cardboard display of cigarette lighters. Boy did my grandfather's voice explode when my uncle suggested we sell them. Still, he frightened no one as, despite his obvious expression of anger, we just couldn't get past those crazy oversized novelty sunglasses he was wearing. Finally, there are also the memories where, by seeing how my grandparents managed the pizza stand, I gained practical experience so important today in running my own business. Heck, how could I ever forget the lesson covering inventory control and open-minded flexibility, or, as we liked to say, "thinking outside the pizza box." One night we ran out of pizza just as the evening rush from the grandstand descended upon us. Desperate – in a Mr. Krabs sort of way – to satisfy all those customers too willing to separate their dollars from their wallets, my grandfather began selling anything not nailed down in the stand. This included all those lighters in the cardboard mounted display my uncle had brought in earlier that day. My grandfather sold the first one before letting my uncle sell the rest.'

As long as the Erie County Fair continues to promote local celebrities (along with the headliners), as long as they continue to feature long-time local vendors (yes, the family pizza stand – now a trailer – remains, operated by my [other] uncle and his family), as long as they continue to feature the arts, crafts and historical exhibits of local creators (alongside the traveling road show of James E. Strates Shows), then I'll be happy knowing future generations will be able to experience a county fair the way past generations have. And this I can guarantee, for, despite all these changes, my own children, who never experienced the same Fair I did growing up, nonetheless look forward to the annual visit to the Fair.

And while every time I step through Gate 2, imagining I'm going back to that old pizza stand, I'm content knowing my children are building their own "River City" memories. On a scale of one to ten, they, like I, rate the Erie County Fair "76 Trombones." But they also have experienced more than just the Hamburg Fair, for Greater Western New York was once and still is filled with these other destinations of amusement.

Footnotes:
[1] Taussig, Ellen, *Reflections of AMERICA'S County Fair, 1841-2000*, Erie County Agricultural Society, 2001, Forward
[2] Ibid., Forward
[3] Ibid., Forward
[4] Ibid., Forward
[5] Ibid., p.1
[6] Ibid., Forward
[7] Ibid., p.2
[8] Ibid., Forward
[9] Ibid., Forward
[10] Ibid.,p.12
[11] Ibid.,p.31
[12] Leary, Thomas E. and Elizabeth C. Sholes, *Buffalo's Pan-American Exposition*, Arcadia Publishing, Charleston, South Carolina, 1998, p. 13
[13] The Erie County Fair web-site, http://www.ecfair.org/about-the-fair/
[14] Taussig, p.31-32

INDEX

ABOUT THE AUTHOR

You might recognize Christopher Carosa as the oft-quoted President of the Bullfinch Fund and its investment adviser Carosa Stanton Asset Management, LLC. A popular and entertaining nationally recognized speaker from coast to coast, he has appeared in, among other media outlets, *The New York Times*, *Barron's*, CNN and Fox Business News.

Mr. Carosa was born in Buffalo and grew up in Hamburg, NY before moving to Chili, NY at age ten. He is a well-known promoter of the Greater Western New York region and also recognized as the local author of the book *50 Hidden Gems of Greater Western New York* (Pandamensional Solutions, 2012) of which he's spoken about to many area service clubs and organizations. He's the first graduate from Gates-Chili High School to attend Yale University. Mr. Carosa has also been a top rated AM disc jockey, at one time was declared one of Rochester's "Most Eligible Bachelors," has climbed to the top of two volcanoes (including Mt. Vesuvius), once earned a national prize for his academic research, has seen a stage play he's written (*The Macaroni Kid*) performed to sold out audiences, and generally has had a pretty good life. Along the way Mr. Carosa has also been a successful serial, some say parallel, entrepreneur. He's created a market research company, a weekly suburban newspaper, a trust company, a mutual fund, and a national media company. Although he does have an MBA from the University of Rochester's prestigious Simon School, Mr. Carosa says he did so only to be able to tell people he didn't need an MBA to be successful in business. In fact, he claims everything he ever learned about business he learned by working in his grandparents' pizza stand at the Erie County Fair.

Mr. Carosa has written four other books: *Hey! What's My Number?* (Pandamensional Solutions, 2014), *401 Fiduciary Solutions* (Pandamensional Solutions, Inc., 2012); *A Life Full of Wonder* (an unpublished novel written in 2005); and, *Due Diligence* (ARDMAN Regional, Ltd., 1999). In addition to other publications, he has written more than 500 articles for *FiduciaryNews.com*.

If you'd like to read more by Mr. Carosa, feel free to browse his author's site, ChrisCarosa.com; LifetimeDreamGuide.com, a site to another book he's working on,; his site devoted to his first love, AstronomyTop100.com, and a site where he, his son, and his daughter offer reviews to classic Hollywood movies, MightyMovieMoments.com.

What he enjoys most is sharing the spell-binding stories of Greater Western New York with family, friends, and fans of the region. Those willing to join him on his crusade to promote all things Greater Western New York are invited to visit GreaterWesternNewYork.com to learn more.

Mr. Carosa lives in Mendon, NY with his wife, Betsy, three children, Cesidia, Catarina, and Peter, and their beagle, Wally.

Check out some reader comments on Chris Carosa's writings about Greater Western New York:

"Chris has displayed a repeated ability to be an 'out of the box' thinker who knows how to convert vision into reality! This book is another example of his unique of abilities!"

- Brian Lipke, Chairman, Gibraltar Industries, Inc. (from the Foreword of *50 Hidden Gems of Greater Western New York*)

"I enjoyed reading this portion of your book. So many Internet articles I find myself skimming over, a consequence of a reduced attention span, but yours kept my interest throughout. Well done!"

- June S.

"Well done, nice reading, great story, lotsa history in Western New York."

- Tony C

"I love your wit, energy and how you know what really is important.... nice job."

- Bob B.

"Interesting article! I've lived in Western New York most of my life and never knew about this. You've got me excited to learn more about Western New York history."

- Jim S.

"Hello Chris. Well Done. I'm a lifetime resident of the Buffalo area. Congrats."

- Nick G.

"Chris – your light-hearted story made me both sad and happy at the same time. I grew up in the Village of Blasdell"

- Pattie P.

"Great Article, Chris! I always wondered what Pre-Emption Road was all about…"

- Dan C.

"I love the tidbits you've been posting – I grew up in Hamburg and am a 5th generation native WNYer…"

- John A.

"I'm ready to secede, NOW."

- Tom B

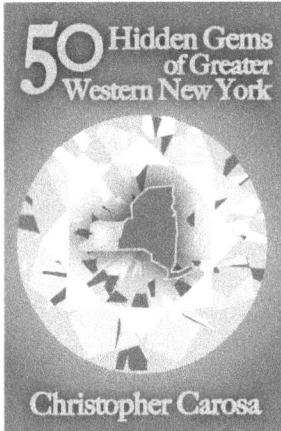

50 Hidden Gems of Greater Western New York

A handbook for those too proud to believe "wide right" and "no goal" define us.

Discover the secrets in your own backyard. For too long the nation has dismissed the Greater Western New York region as a mere punch-line. That ends now. *50 Hidden Gems of Greater Western New York*, in a light-hearted and entertaining manner, reveals some of the most delicious underexposed treasures our region offers. These people, places and events not only help define Greater Western New York, but have often helped define America as well. Don't, however, underestimate the power of this collection of witty stories. Rather than a mere historical review eulogizing the faded glory of what once was, *50 Hidden Gems of Greater Western New York* takes you on an expedition celebrating the rich character of our region. In doing so, the discerning reader will unearth perhaps the most powerful hidden gem of them all: the key to Greater Western New York's future success.

Along the journey, you'll discover:

- A controversial early-American whose actions led directly to the creation of the U.S. Constitution.
- Our region's claim to be the origin of America's favorite fast food (and, no, we're not talking Buffalo Wings).
- The home of the Grand Canyon of the East.
- The fascinating story of the mysterious Lost Tribe of Western New York.
- A Rochester-born woman who holds this Hollywood first – that almost wasn't.
- The time a small Western New York hamlet seceded from the Union – and its ensuing oversight.
- The truth behind the story of New York State's smallest town's eerie tragedy.
- How the bumbling British Monarchy helped mark the borders of Greater Western New York.

www.ingramcontent.com/pod-product-compliance
Lightning Source LLC
Chambersburg PA
CBHW062034200326
41519CB00017B/5033